VERDURE!

Vegetables the Italian Way

Text by Elisabetta Lotti
Photography by Marco Lanza
Set Design by Elisabetta Lotti

McRae Books

© 1997 McRae Books Srl, Florence (Italy)

Conceived, edited, and designed by McRae Books
Publishers: Anne McRae, Marco Nardi

Text: Elisabetta Lotti
Photography: Marco Lanza
Set Design: Elisabetta Lotti
Design: Marco Nardi

Translation from the Italian: Executive Service
Editing: Alison Leach and Anne McRae
Color separations: Fotolito Toscana, Florence, Italy

The publishers would like to thank Coin (Florence) and Bartolini (Florence)
for their assistance during the production of this book.

ISBN 88-900126-1-7

Printed and bound in Italy by Artegrafica, Verona

CONTENTS

INTRODUCTION

*Every season brings its harvest of fresh,
life-giving vegetables. Cooking and preparing them for
family and friends is always satisfying. Not only
will the results of your labors be greeted with pleasure
and healthy appetites, but you will be serene in the
knowledge that you are doing your guests a good
turn. Vegetables are overflowing with essential
vitamins, minerals, and fiber, and along with fruit,
should be one of the mainstays of a healthy diet.
Fortunately, Italy's Mediterranean climate ensures a
well-stocked vegetable cupboard year round, and its
long and justly famous culinary tradition contains a
rich store of recipes for all seasons and every occasion.
To introduce even novice cooks to a part of this
tradition, I have divided the book into five chapters
based on the ways the vegetables are prepared, preceded
by an introductory section on recognizing and
choosing vegetables, preparing and cooking them, and
the basic utensils and sauces required. Most recipes
finish with one or more serving suggestions. These are
only intended as guidelines; all the dishes in this book
can be served in myriad ways. Experiment a little,
and find them all out! Buon appetito!*

VEGETABLES

For those of us without green fingers or a garden, the vegetables we eat will be bought at a supermarket or market. If you have the choice, buy at a market where the vegetables will be fresher. In Italy, many small farmers bring their products into the market squares fresh from the fields every morning, which is almost as good as having your own garden! When buying vegetables, quality and freshness are of utmost importance. Generally speaking, products should be firm to touch, with good color, and no withered or yellowing leaves. Experience is the best guide, so examine the vegetables you buy closely to learn what each one should look like to taste good. Another important rule is that all vegetables need to be very thoroughly washed in abundant cold running water before you begin preparing them.

ARTICHOKES

Choose artichokes with plump heads and tightly folded leaves. Young artichokes can be eaten raw; the maturer ones are better cooked. Only the inner leaves and heart are edible. To clean an artichoke, remove all but the pale inner leaves by pulling the outer ones down and snapping them off. Cut off the stem at the base of the head and the top third of the leaves. Cut the artichokes in half lengthwise and scrape any fuzzy choke away with a knife. Soak them in a bowl of cold water with the juice of 1 lemon for 10 minutes to stop them turning black.

ASPARAGUS

The asparagus season is mid-spring to early summer, although nowadays specialty markets keep imported ones all year round. Often expensive, it pays to choose them with care. They should be firm, with well-formed, compact stalks. Beware of wilting stalks or woody stems. Asparagus should be cooked and eaten as soon as possible. Trim the tough parts off the stems, wash well, and cook in (or steam over) a pot of salted, boiling water until tender.

GREEN BEANS

Also known as French beans, they are best in spring and summer. They should be bright green with no blemishes or spots. Snap the end off one between your thumb and forefinger; if fresh, the bean will break easily. To prepare, cut the ends off and wash well.

PEAS

Fresh green peas appear in the markets in spring and summer. The younger they are, the sweeter they will be. Choose those with plump, bright green pods. They should be eaten as soon as possible. During the rest of the year frozen peas are an acceptable substitute and widely available.

FAVA BEANS (Broad beans)

Fava beans are in season from early spring to midsummer. Buy them when their pods are bright green and crisp. In Italy, very young fava beans are eaten raw with a little salt, Pecorino cheese, or salami. The maturer beans can be cooked in many different ways. They are also available in frozen and dried forms.

BROCCOLI

Broccoli is now available all year round, but it is best in fall and winter. Choose deep-green broccoli with tightly closed florets. Broccoli stem is also tasty; peel and dice it. It takes longer to cook than the florets. Broccoli can be cooked in a variety of ways; one of the best is to stir-fry it with olive oil, salt, and crushed chilies. Serve as a sauce over large, dry pasta shapes.

CAULIFLOWER

Traditionally a winter vegetable, it is now available throughout the year. The white head should show no blemishing or discoloring and the leaves should be fresh and unwilted. Remove the leaves to cook and divide the head into florets. The stalk is also tasty but takes longer to cook than the florets. Peel it, dice it up, and add to the pot 5 minutes before the florets.

PUMPKIN

There are many varieties available all year round, although they are generally better in fall and winter. Often sold in pieces, make sure that they are unblemished, with no soft spots. If buying a whole pumpkin, choose one with a glossy skin which feels heavy. Pumpkin keeps in the refrigerator for several days. It can be boiled, steamed, baked, roasted, or fried.

ZUCCHINI

Their natural season is fall to autumn, although they are now available all year round. Zucchini should be firm to touch, with glossy, blemish-free skins. They are at their peak in early summer and can be eaten raw then. In Italy, zucchini blossoms are considered a delicacy. Buy the male flowers that grow on a stem, and not the female ones which are attached to the end of the zucchini. The blossoms are usually dipped in batter (see recipe p. 20) and fried for a few minutes in oil. Sprinkled with salt, they make a tasty appetizer. Sprinkled with sugar, they are a delicious dessert.

CABBAGE

There are many different varieties of cabbage, including Savoy, red, or the common pale green type. Normally a winter vegetable, some varieties also grow during spring and summer. Most cabbages have tightly packed leaves and will keep in the refrigerator for 4–5 days. Remove the tough stem and wilted outer leaves and cut or chop the vegetable as required. Cabbage can be eaten raw, or cooked in a variety of ways.

BRUSSELS SPROUTS

These tiny cabbages grow in fall and winter. Buy them fresh, firm, and bright green in color. They will keep for 2-3 days in the refrigerator in a plastic bag. Trim the stems, remove the outer leaves, and rinse thoroughly under cold running water. Cook them in salted, boiling water for 7–8 minutes. Don't overcook or they will turn mushy and tasteless.

SALAD BURNET
One of the many small salad greens commonly available in Italy. Corn salad, cress, wild endives, and lollo rosso are also popular. Choose local varieties of crisp, fresh greens.

SPINACH
Available from fall to spring. Choose young, tender spinach with crisp, deep-green leaves. Separate the leaves and wash very thoroughly. Frozen spinach is an acceptable substitute in summer.

ARUGULA (Rocket)
This pleasantly peppery salad green grows from spring to fall. Choose crisp, dark-green arugula, with unblemished leaves. It will keep a day or two in a plastic bag in the refrigerator.

ESCAROLE
Another member of the chicory family. Buy escarole only when it its open wavy leaves, with their pale-green ruffled tips, are crisp and unwilted. The heart can be used in salads, while the leaves have a pleasant, earthy taste when cooked.

RADICCHIO
There are several types of round or long red radicchio available in Italy throughout the year. They are all more or less bitter in taste and can be served either raw in salads, or baked or grilled. There are also many varieties of small green radicchio (both wild and cultivated). They are usually served in salads.

BELGIAN ENDIVE
Also known as French endive. Another member of the chicory family. Choose white, well-closed heads and store them in the dark—the light will turn the leaves green. Clean by removing the outer leaves and chopping the tough part off the bottom. Serve in salads or cooked.

CATALONIA
Part of the chicory family, this is a bitter cooking green with long, tapering leaves, white at the bottom and dark green toward the tops. Choose compact, unwilted heads. If you enjoy bracing bitter flavors, serve it boiled or steamed, dressed with a little olive oil and lemon juice.

LETTUCE
There are many different types of lettuce available throughout the year. Common cutting lettuce is usually round, with pale green and white leaves folded over each other. The central white heart is the best part. Romaine lettuce has elongated dark green leaves. Choose lettuces with crisp well-colored leaves. Trim the bottoms, detach the leaves, and wash accurately.

SWISS CHARD
The dwarf varieties are sweeter and lack the large white stalk of the larger ones. They can be served raw in salads or cooked. The large stalks are nearly always cooked. Choose fresh, bright green heads with crisp leaves.

ONIONS
There are many types of onions available throughout the year. The large white and yellow varieties are used to flavor many cooked dishes, while the large red variety is sweet enough to be served (thinly sliced) in salads. Squeeze onions before you buy them to make sure they are not rotting beneath their skins.

BABY ONIONS
White, baby onions can be pickled, grilled, or served in sweet and sour sauces.

LEEKS
A member of the onion family. Trim off the green tops and roots, and peel the outer layers of the central white stalk. Although sometimes served in salads, their strong flavor makes them more suitable for cooking. Buy them with their green tops, which should be fresh-looking and unwilted.

SCALLIONS
(Spring onions)
Available from early spring to fall. Trim the tops and bottoms, peel off the outer layers of white skin, and chop into salads.

FENNEL
With its mild taste of aniseed, fennel is a refreshing salad vegetable. It can also be braised, sautéed, baked, or fried. Only the bulb is used; the stalks and leaves are usually discarded. Available year round, its natural season is winter and spring. Generally speaking, the plump bulbs are best in salads, while the longer, flatter ones are better cooked.

CELERY
Choose fresh, crisp heads of celery with bright white stalks and unwilted green leaves. Use only the inner stalks and hearts in salads. To cook, remove the strings from the larger, outer stalks before chopping.

CARDOONS
Cardoons taste like artichokes, although they look more like a head of celery to buy. Choose crisp, unwilted heads. Trim the tops, strip off the outer, bitter-tasting leaves and serve raw or cooked.

RADISHES
Available throughout the year. Try to buy them with their tops attached, since these will show how fresh they are. Cut off the roots and tops, wash well, and serve the tiny red bulbs in salads, or by themselves (with a dish of salt handy for dipping).

CARROTS
Carrots are available throughout the year. Baby carrots are often sold with their tops; if the leaves are bright green and unwilted the carrots will be fresh. Choose older carrots carefully; they should be bright orange in color, well-shaped, and firm. Scrub well or peel before use.

CHERRY TOMATOES
In season, tiny cherry tomatoes are packed with flavor.

TOMATOES
The tomato is ubiquitous in Italian cuisine. Fresh tomatoes are now available year round, although the outdoor, summer varieties have an unbeatable flavor. Canned tomatoes are an acceptable substitute for fresh ones in sauces and soups during the winter months.

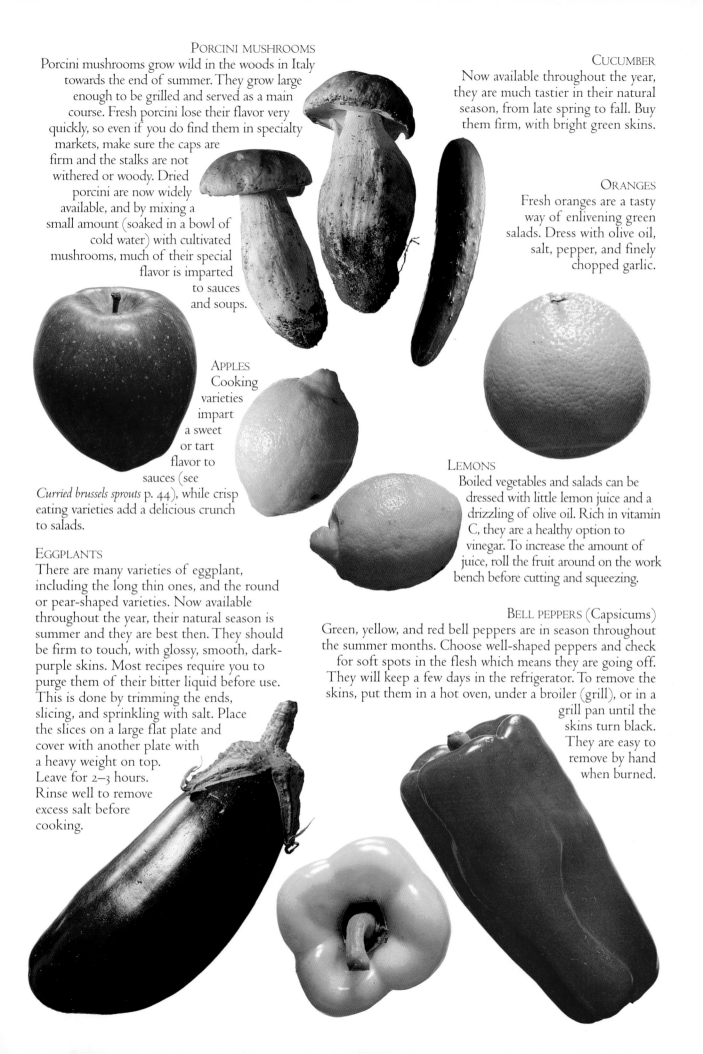

PORCINI MUSHROOMS

Porcini mushrooms grow wild in the woods in Italy towards the end of summer. They grow large enough to be grilled and served as a main course. Fresh porcini lose their flavor very quickly, so even if you do find them in specialty markets, make sure the caps are firm and the stalks are not withered or woody. Dried porcini are now widely available, and by mixing a small amount (soaked in a bowl of cold water) with cultivated mushrooms, much of their special flavor is imparted to sauces and soups.

CUCUMBER

Now available throughout the year, they are much tastier in their natural season, from late spring to fall. Buy them firm, with bright green skins.

ORANGES

Fresh oranges are a tasty way of enlivening green salads. Dress with olive oil, salt, pepper, and finely chopped garlic.

APPLES

Cooking varieties impart a sweet or tart flavor to sauces (see *Curried brussels sprouts* p. 44), while crisp eating varieties add a delicious crunch to salads.

LEMONS

Boiled vegetables and salads can be dressed with little lemon juice and a drizzling of olive oil. Rich in vitamin C, they are a healthy option to vinegar. To increase the amount of juice, roll the fruit around on the work bench before cutting and squeezing.

EGGPLANTS

There are many varieties of eggplant, including the long thin ones, and the round or pear-shaped varieties. Now available throughout the year, their natural season is summer and they are best then. They should be firm to touch, with glossy, smooth, dark-purple skins. Most recipes require you to purge them of their bitter liquid before use. This is done by trimming the ends, slicing, and sprinkling with salt. Place the slices on a large flat plate and cover with another plate with a heavy weight on top. Leave for 2–3 hours. Rinse well to remove excess salt before cooking.

BELL PEPPERS (Capsicums)

Green, yellow, and red bell peppers are in season throughout the summer months. Choose well-shaped peppers and check for soft spots in the flesh which means they are going off. They will keep a few days in the refrigerator. To remove the skins, put them in a hot oven, under a broiler (grill), or in a grill pan until the skins turn black. They are easy to remove by hand when burned.

HERBS, SPICES, AND COOKING TIPS

Fresh herbs will add extra zest and flavor to everything you cook, whether it be Italian or not. Most common herbs are now readily available at markets. If you can't find fresh herbs, use them in dried form. Remember to store dried herbs in airtight containers and to buy new supplies regularly, so that they don't loose all their flavor.

BASIL

MINT

CHERVIL

HOW TO BROIL (GRILL) VEGETABLES

Broiling or grilling vegetables is a traditional cooking method in Italy. For best results indoors, you will need a basic grill pan. You can also successfully grill vegetables over a barbecue, in the same way that meat is cooked. The most suitable vegetables are bell peppers, eggplant, mushrooms, red radicchio, zucchini, fennel, tomatoes, and onions.

There are only two basic rules:

• Choose only top-quality vegetables.

• Temperature: heat the grill pan to very hot before placing the vegetables in it. This stops them from sticking to the pan and cooks them quickly (so that they won't have time to dry out).

And many advantages:

• Simplicity and speed: the vegetables only need to be washed and chopped. You can grill a good selection of vegetables in about 30 minutes. The result will be an attractive and delicious entrée or side dish for 4–6 people.

• Health: grilling vegetables not only enhances their natural flavors, it also maintains most of their vitamins and minerals intact.

• Low fat: the vegetables are grilled without oil, butter, or fats of any kind. You can choose how much oil to add when serving.

• Preparing ahead of time: when the vegetables are grilled, you can either drizzle with olive oil and serve them hot, or let cool and sprinkle with freshly chopped herbs (garlic, parsley, mint, oregano, and others). Dress with oil and serve later in the day. Well-covered with oil, bell peppers and eggplants will keep for about a week in the refrigerator.

FLAT-LEAF PARSLEY

TARRAGON

DILL

CHIVES

How to Fry Vegetables

To obtain perfect results when frying vegetables you will need a deep-sided skillet or frying pan, a slotted spoon, tongs (or two forks), and abundant high-quality oil. Fried dishes should be eaten hot; serve them as you cook or as soon afterward as possible. Prepare the vegetables and batter ahead. Basic rules for successful frying are:

• Oil: olive oil is one of the best oils for frying. It resists heat well and leaves no taste on the food. Sunflower oil is also good.

• Temperature: don't begin frying before the oil is hot enough. Initially, you may prefer to use a thermometer to gauge heat. Ideal cooking temperatures are:
Moderate (300°F/150°C): ideal for larger pieces of raw vegetable that need time to cook;
Hot (325°F/160°C): ideal for precooked vegetables and croquettes;
Very hot (350°F/180°C): ideal for vegetables in julienne strips, leaves, or tiny pieces of vegetables that require instant frying.
Otherwise, check temperature by putting a small piece of the vegetable you wish to fry in the oil to see how it reacts and adjust temperature accordingly. Temperature should never exceed 350°F (180°C). Don't wait until the oil is smoking; this is dangerous as the oil may catch fire (if it does, don't use water to extinguish it, just turn off the electricity or gas and cover the pan with a lid).

• Always use plenty of oil. The vegetables should be floating when you add them to the pan so that their surfaces seal immediately against the oil. The less oil that enters the surface, the lighter and healthier the finished dish will be.

• Never use the same oil more than once. During cooking, keep the oil clean; if you leave tiny pieces of batter or vegetable in the pan, they will burn and their acrid flavor will contaminate the taste of the other vegetables. Keep the oil topped up to the same level during cooking.

• The vegetables you want to fry should be at room temperature. If they are too cold, they will take longer to heat and absorb more oil.

• Don't put too many pieces in the pan at once. They will lower the temperature of the oil, increasing cooking time and amount of oil absorbed. They may also stick together in a single unappetizing lump.

• If you are using a wire basket, heat it in the oil before adding the vegetables to prevent them from sticking to it.

GARLIC

BLACK PEPPERCORNS

SHALLOTS

SAGE

CHILIES

OREGANO

THYME   CALAMINT   ROSEMARY

BAY LEAVES

MEATS, CHEESES, OIL, AND VINEGAR

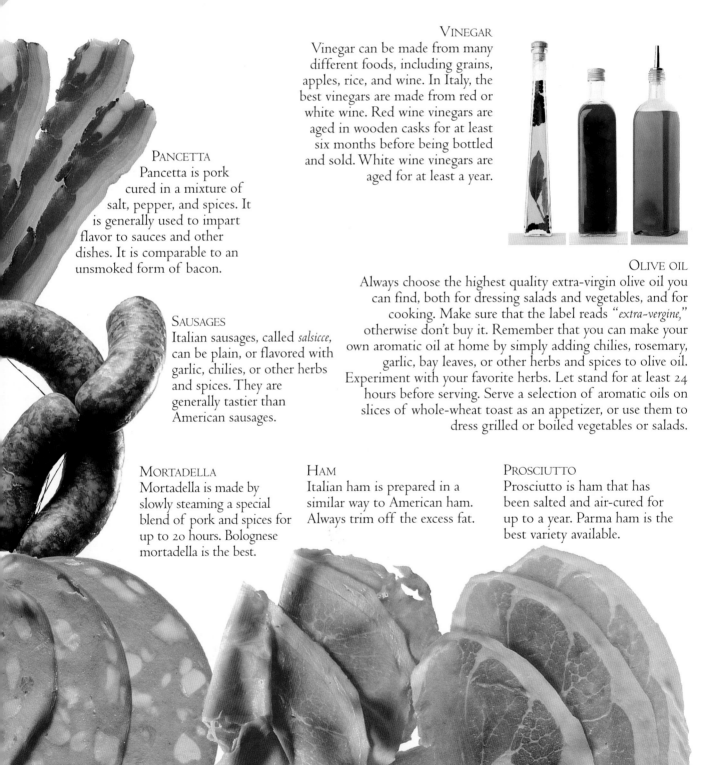

Many of the dishes in this book are prepared using ingredients that are specific to the Italian pantry. Due to the success of Italian cuisine abroad, most are now widely available in supermarkets and food stores. You may need to look for some of the cheeses in specialty stores. If you can't find the exact Italian ingredient, read the description carefully and look for a similar local product. Olive oil is the only ingredient that can't be substituted with another.

VINEGAR
Vinegar can be made from many different foods, including grains, apples, rice, and wine. In Italy, the best vinegars are made from red or white wine. Red wine vinegars are aged in wooden casks for at least six months before being bottled and sold. White wine vinegars are aged for at least a year.

PANCETTA
Pancetta is pork cured in a mixture of salt, pepper, and spices. It is generally used to impart flavor to sauces and other dishes. It is comparable to an unsmoked form of bacon.

OLIVE OIL
Always choose the highest quality extra-virgin olive oil you can find, both for dressing salads and vegetables, and for cooking. Make sure that the label reads *"extra-vergine,"* otherwise don't buy it. Remember that you can make your own aromatic oil at home by simply adding chilies, rosemary, garlic, bay leaves, or other herbs and spices to olive oil. Experiment with your favorite herbs. Let stand for at least 24 hours before serving. Serve a selection of aromatic oils on slices of whole-wheat toast as an appetizer, or use them to dress grilled or boiled vegetables or salads.

SAUSAGES
Italian sausages, called *salsicce*, can be plain, or flavored with garlic, chilies, or other herbs and spices. They are generally tastier than American sausages.

MORTADELLA
Mortadella is made by slowly steaming a special blend of pork and spices for up to 20 hours. Bolognese mortadella is the best.

HAM
Italian ham is prepared in a similar way to American ham. Always trim off the excess fat.

PROSCIUTTO
Prosciutto is ham that has been salted and air-cured for up to a year. Parma ham is the best variety available.

FONTINA WEDGE
For the cheese board.

FONTINA
Tasty cheese originally from the Valle d'Aosta in the foothills and Alps of northern Italy. Made from cow's milk, it is ideal both for cooking and the cheese board.

FONTINA SLICES
Ideal for cooking.

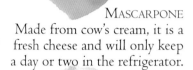

MOZZARELLA
Traditionally made from buffalo milk. Many good quality varieties are now made from cow's milk.

MASCARPONE
Made from cow's cream, it is a fresh cheese and will only keep a day or two in the refrigerator.

PROVOLONE
Provolone cheese is made from cow's milk. In Italy it comes in an amazing variety of forms, from tiny pear-like shapes to gigantic cylinders. It has a thin golden brown crust. There are two main types—*dolce* (mild) and *piccante* (tasty). Tasty provolone is ideal for flavoring dishes. Grate over the top as with parmesan or pecorino.

PECORINO
Tasty *pecorino romano*, made from ewe's milk and carefully aged, is best for grating over baked dishes. The younger varieties can be eaten fresh.

PARMIGIANO
Parmesan is made from cow's milk aged for at least 18 months. Buy in wedges and grate fresh as required.

CAPRINO
A delicate, slightly tart fresh cheese made of goat milk, or a mixture of goat and cow's milk.

GRUYÈRE AND EMMENTHAL
From Switzerland, France, and Holland, they are widely used in Italian cookery.

RICOTTA
Delicate fresh cheese made of goat, ewe's, or cow's milk.

BASIC SAUCES

Ragù di carni miste
Meat sauce

Ragù is a tomato-based sauce made with meat and chopped vegetables and spices. It is one of the classic pasta sauces, but is also very good with many vegetable recipes, particularly baked dishes. Because making a ragù is a time-consuming business (and also because it will keep in the refrigerator for about a week and in the freezer for several months), the recipe below is for 10-12 portions.

Serves 10-12; Preparation: 1 hour; Cooking: 2½ hours; Level of difficulty: Simple

Place 3 tablespoons of oil, 3 cloves of garlic, the sage, rosemary, beef, pork, chicken and sausages in a large heavy-bottomed pan and cook for 15 minutes, stirring frequently with a wooden spoon. § When the meat is almost cooked (browned, with no red blood visible), remove from the pan, drain and set aside on a plate. § Discard the sage and rosemary and add the carrots, onion, celery and the rest of the garlic and oil. Stir well to amalgamate and cook for 5-10 minutes. § In the meantime, chop the meat finely in an electric blender or with a sharp knife. § Pour the wine over the vegetables and cook for 10 more minutes. § Add the meat and brandy and cook until the brandy evaporates. § Add the milk and simmer for 5 minutes, then add the tomatoes. § Season with salt and pepper, turn the heat to medium-low, and simmer, partially covered, for about 2 hours. § Stir the sauce from time to time so that it doesn't stick to the bottom of the pan. § After 1½ hours, add the basil and taste to see if there is enough salt. § If, after 2 hours, the ragù is too watery, uncover and simmer for 10-15 minutes more. § When cooked, add the butter and remove from the heat.

■ INGREDIENTS

- 1 cup (8 fl oz/250 ml) extra-virgin olive oil
- 5 cloves garlic, finely chopped
- 1 sprig fresh sage
- 2 twigs fresh rosemary
- 10 oz (300 g) lean beef, coarsely chopped
- 14 oz (450 g) lean pork, coarsely chopped
- 1 large chicken breast, boneless and coarsely chopped
- 2 Italian pork sausages, skinned and crumbled
- 2 large carrots, 1 large onion, 2 large stalks celery, all finely chopped
- 1¼ cups (10 fl oz/300 ml) dry white wine
- 1 cup (8 fl oz/250 ml) brandy
- 2 cups (16 fl oz/500 ml) milk
- 3½ lb (1.8 kg) tomatoes
- salt and black pepper
- 40 leaves basil, torn
- 1½ oz (45 g) butter

Salsa di pomodoro semplice
Basic tomato sauce

Tomato sauce is another classic for pasta, but it is very versatile and can be used in many other dishes, including those based on vegetables, eggs, or meat. If you use fresh tomatoes, you will need to cook the sauce a little longer (about 25 minutes), because of the water they release during cooking. Needless to say, fresh tomatoes produce the tastiest results. Add a knob of butter at the end for a sweeter sauce.

Serves 4; Preparation: 5 minutes; Cooking: 15-20 minutes; Level of difficulty: Simple

Cook the garlic in a sauté pan with the oil until golden, remove from the pan, and add the tomatoes. Season with salt and pepper to taste and cook over medium heat. § Add the basil 5 minutes before the sauce is cooked. § If the sauce is still too watery, turn up the heat until it reduces sufficiently.

■ INGREDIENTS

- 3 cloves garlic, cut in half
- 4 tablespoons extra-virgin olive oil
- 1 lb (500 g) peeled and chopped fresh or canned tomatoes
- salt and freshly ground black pepper
- 10 leaves fresh basil

Right:
Ragù di carni miste

Plain pastry

■ INGREDIENTS

- 2½ cups (8 oz/250 g) all-purpose (plain) flour
- 2 teaspoons salt
- 1 egg yolk
- ½ cup (4 oz/125 g) butter, at room temperature, thinly sliced
- 2 tablespoons water

Makes: pastry to line and cover a 10-in (25-cm) pan; Preparation: 10 minutes + 30 minutes to chill

Combine the flour in a large bowl with the salt. Make a hollow in the center and fill with the egg, butter, and water. Mix the ingredients with a fork, mashing the butter as you work. § After 2–3 minutes the dough will have absorbed almost all the flour. It should be quite crumbly. § Transfer to a lightly floured work surface and shape into a soft compact ball, kneading as little as possible. § Place in a springform pan or pie plate and flatten a little. Using the heels of your palms and your fingertips, spread the dough so that it covers the base of the pan and three-quarters of the sides evenly. Use a fork to shape the sides and bring to the same height. § Cover with plastic wrap and chill in the refrigerator for at least 30 minutes. § This pastry can be prepared a few hours ahead, or even the day before.

Pasta sfoglia
Puff pastry

If this pastry is being used for a sweet dessert, dissolve a dash of sugar in the water.

■ INGREDIENTS

- 2 cups (7 oz/200 g) all-purpose (plain) flour
- dash of salt
- about 1 cup (8 fl oz/ 250 ml) water
- 1 cup (8 oz/250 g) butter, softened
- dash of sugar (optional)

Serves: 4-6; Preparation: 50 minutes + 30 minutes to rest; Level of difficulty: Complicated

Sift the flour and salt in a mound on a clean work surface, make a well in the center, and pour about half the water into it. Using your hands, mix the ingredients until the dough is about the same consistency as the softened butter. Adjust the dough to achieve the required consistency by adding flour or water. § Roll the dough into a ball, wrap in plastic wrap and set aside for 30 minutes. § Use a rolling pin to roll the dough out on a floured work surface into a square shape until about ½ in (1 cm) thick. § Cut the softened butter in pieces and place them at the center of the square. Fold the 4 sides of the square so that the butter is completely sealed in, and roll the dough out in a rectangular shape about ½ in (1 cm) thick. § Fold the rectangle in 3, turn the folded dough, and roll it out again. Fold it again and let stand for about 10 minutes. § Repeat this operation 3 times, letting the dough rest each time for 10 minutes. § Roll out to ¼ in (1 cm) thickness and use as indicated.

Right:
Preparing plain pastry

BRODO DI VERDURE
Vegetable stock

Vegetable stock is an essential ingredient in many soups and risotti. Vegetarians can use it in recipes that call for chicken or beef stock. For a completely fat-free stock, omit the butter and put all the ingredients together in the lightly salted water, and simmer for about 1 hour.

Makes: 3½ quarts (7 pints/3½ liters); Preparation: 15 minutes; Cooking: 1¼ hours; Level of difficulty: Simple

Melt the butter in a fairly large pot and add the vegetables. Cover and simmer over low heat for 10 minutes, stirring occasionally. § Add the parsley, peppercorns, cloves, bay leaf, and season with salt. § Add the water and simmer for 1 hour over low heat, skimming off the foam occasionally. § Strain the stock, discarding the vegetables.

■ INGREDIENTS

- 4 tablespoons butter
- 2 onions, 2 carrots, 1 leek, 2 stalks celery with leaves, cut in 4 pieces
- 3 tomatoes, cut in half
- 6 sprigs parsley
- 8 black peppercorns
- 1 clove
- 1 bay leaf (optional)
- dash of salt
- 4 quarts (8 pints/4 liters) cold water

BRODO DI CARNE
Beef stock

Homemade beef stock is used as the basis for many soups, to serve filled pasta such as tortellini and agnolotti, and to flavor a wide range of other pasta and risotto dishes. It can be made ahead of time and kept in the refrigerator for up to 3 days or frozen.

Makes: about 2 quarts (4 pints/2 liters); Preparation: 15 minutes; Cooking: 3 hours; Level of difficulty: Simple

Put the meat, vegetables, herbs, salt, and pepper in a large pot with the water. Cover and bring to a boil over medium heat. Simmer over low heat for 3 hours. Skim the foam off the top at intervals so that the stock will be light and fresh to taste. § Remove from heat and leave to cool. When the stock is cool, a layer of fat will form on the top. This should be skimmed off.

■ INGREDIENTS

- 2 lb (1 kg) beef
- 2 lb (1 kg) meat bones
- 1 carrot
- 1 onion
- 1 stalk celery
- 1 whole clove
- 1 bay leaf
- 1 clove garlic
- 5 sprigs parsley
- 1 leek
- 1 ripe tomato
- salt and freshly ground black pepper
- 2½ quarts (5 pints/ 2.5 liters) water

PASTELLA PER FRIGGERE
Batter

Serves 4; Preparation: 45 minutes; Level of difficulty: Simple

Sift the flour into a medium-sized mixing bowl, make a hole at the center and add the egg yolk. § Add the oil and salt and stir in the water a little at a time to obtain a thick but fluid batter without lumps. Set aside for 30–40 minutes. § Just before frying, stir the batter well, beat the egg white until stiff and fold it gently into the batter. Use the batter as indicated in the recipes.

■ INGREDIENTS

- 1 cup (4 oz/125 g) all-purpose (plain) flour
- 1 egg, separated
- 1 tablespoon extra-virgin olive oil
- dash of salt
- cold water

Right: Brodo di carne

CRESPELLE
Crêpes

*Crêpes are small pancakes made with milk, egg, and flour. They are never eaten
on their own but are used as the basis for countless sweet and savory recipes.*

*Makes: 10-12 crêpes; Preparation: 10 minutes + 2 hours to rest; Cooking: 30 minutes; Level of
difficulty: Simple*

Beat the eggs, sugar, and salt with the sifted flour. § Pour in the milk
gradually, followed by the melted butter. Beat the batter until smooth
then set aside to rest for 2 hours. § Brush a small, heated skillet (frying
pan) with the remaining butter, and add a small ladleful of batter.
Spread evenly by tipping the pan, so that it forms a thin film. Cook the
crêpe on both sides, taking care not to let it color too much. When the
edges curl slightly, it is done. § If not using immediately, crêpes can be stored in
the refrigerator, piled one on top of the other in a covered container.

VARIATIONS
– Flavor the batter with two tablespoonfuls of rum or cognac.
– Other types of flour can also be used in the making of crêpes,
such as buckwheat or whole-wheat.

■ INGREDIENTS

• 2 eggs
• 1 teaspoon sugar
• dash of salt
• 1 cup (4 oz/125 g)
  all-purpose (plain) flour
• 1 cup (8 fl oz/250 ml)
  milk
• 1½ tablespoons butter,
  melted, plus 1 teaspoon
  butter, at room
  temperature, to grease
  the pan

SALSA BESCIAMELLA
Béchamel sauce

*Béchamel sauce is a basic ingredient in many baked vegetable dishes. Always make a generous
amount when using the sauce with vegetables because it is difficult to predict how much they will
absorb. If you make too much, use it to revive leftover vegetables (or pasta) by combining them with
the béchamel in an ovenproof dish (with a little tomato sauce, if you have it). Sprinkle with freshly
grated Parmesan cheese and bake for 15 minutes in a hot oven.*

Serves: 4; Preparation: 5 minutes; Cooking: 7-8 minutes; Level of difficulty: Simple

Heat the milk in a saucepan until it is almost boiling. § In a heavy-bottomed
saucepan, melt the butter with the flour over low heat, stirring rapidly with
a wooden spoon. Cook for about 1 minute. § Remove from heat and add
half the hot milk, stirring constantly. Return to low heat and stir until the
sauce starts to thicken. § Add the rest of the milk gradually and continue
stirring until it comes to a boil. § Season with salt to taste and continue stirring until the béchamel is the right thickness. § If any lumps form, beat the
sauce rapidly with a fork or whisk until they dissolve.

■ INGREDIENTS

• 2 cups (16 fl oz/500 ml)
  milk
• 4 tablespoons butter
• ½ cup (2 oz/60 g) all-
  purpose (plain) flour
• dash of salt

Right: *Salsa besciamella*

Salsa maionese
Mayonnaise

Making mayonnaise is not easy at first, but with a little patience you will master the art and homemade mayonnaise is so much better than the store-bought variety, that it really is worth the effort. The best results are achieved by hand, but I have also included instructions for making it in a blender.

Serves: 4; Preparation: 15-20 minutes; Level of difficulty: Medium

BY HAND: use a fork or hand whisk to beat the egg yolk in a bowl with the salt. § Add the oil a drop at a time at first, then in a steady drizzle, stirring all the time in the same direction. § When the mayonnaise begins to thicken, add, very gradually, the lemon juice (or vinegar), pepper, and a few more drops of oil until it is the right density. § If the mayonnaise curdles, start over again with another egg yolk and use the curdled mayonnaise in place of the oil.

IN THE BLENDER: use the same ingredients as above, except for the egg, which should be whole. § Place the egg, salt, pepper, 1–2 tablespoons of oil, and the lemon juice (or vinegar) in the blender and blend for a few seconds at maximum speed. § When the ingredients are well mixed, pour the remaining oil into the mixture very gradually. Blend until the right density is reached.

Salsa vinaigrette
Vinaigrette (Salad dressing)

Serves: 4; Preparation: 10 minutes; Level of difficulty: Simple

Put the vinegar in a bowl and dissolve the salt in it. § Add the oil and pepper and beat with a whisk or fork to emulsify.

VARIATIONS
– Vary the basic vinaigrette salad dressing by adding other ingredients to taste; for example, finely chopped garlic; onion; spring onions; crispy-fried diced pancetta; fresh raw egg yolk; or anchovy paste (in this case leave out the salt) with chopped hard-boiled egg and a clove of finely chopped garlic.
– Add another tablespoon of oil and 100 g (3½ oz) of crumbled Gorgonzola cheese to the basic mixture. Mix well to obtain a creamy sauce.
– Add a teaspoon of mild or strong mustard (whichever you prefer) to the basic dressing, or a teaspoon of mustard seeds. Marinate for at least 30 minutes before serving.
– Adding aromatic herbs to the basic dressing is the easiest way to flavor the dressing. Some favorite herbs are: mint, thyme, oregano, chives, or chervil.

Right:
Homemade mayonnaise

Braised and Sautéed Vegetables

Almost all vegetables can be braised or sautéed. The idea is to exalt the flavors of the main ingredient without overwhelming it. The authentic recipes in this chapter are only a tiny portion of the full Italian repertoire. Once you have mastered these, use your imagination and personal tastes to invent others.

Zucchine intere ripiene
Stuffed zucchini

*If there is any left-over filling, roll it into walnut-sized balls, flour lightly
and fry until golden brown. Serve with the filled zucchini.*

Serves: 4; Preparation: 30-40 minutes; Cooking: 40 minutes; Level of difficulty: Simple

Cut the zucchini in half, remove the pulp and set it aside. § Mix the pork,
sausage, mortadella, Parmesan, parsley, garlic, eggs, salt, and pepper in a bowl.
Use a fork to blend the mixture thoroughly. § Stuff the hollowed-out
zucchini with the filling. § Heat the frying oil in a sauté pan and fry the
stuffed zucchini halves for 2–3 minutes. Drain on paper towels. § To make the
sauce, pour the olive oil and tomatoes into a large skillet (frying pan), add
4–5 tablespoons of zucchini pulp, basil, and salt and pepper to taste. Cook
over medium heat for 5 minutes. § Place the stuffed zucchini in the skillet
with the sauce and add 1 cup (8 fl oz/250 ml) of water. Cook for 20 minutes
covered with a sheet of aluminum foil with a small hole in it for the steam to
escape. Uncover, and cook for 10 minutes more or until the sauce has
reduced. § Serve hot on a bed of Parmesan or saffron risotto.

> VARIATION
> – For a spicier filling, use Pecorino romano cheese instead of
> Parmesan, and finely chopped prosciutto instead of mortadella.

Zucchine trifolate
Braised zucchini

Serves: 4: Preparation: 10 minutes; Cooking: 10-15 minutes; Level of difficulty: Simple

Cut the cloves of garlic in two and place them in a skillet (frying pan) with
the oil. Sauté over medium heat until the garlic turns light gold. § Remove
the garlic, add the butter and zucchini, and cook over high heat for 5 minutes. § Reduce heat to medium-low, cover, and simmer for 5 more minutes.
§ Season with salt and pepper, uncover, and complete cooking. Don't let the
zucchini turn mushy; the wheels should stay whole. § Remove from heat,
add the parsley, toss well, and transfer to a heated serving dish.

> VARIATIONS
> – Replace the parsley with 1 tablespoon of finely chopped fresh
> mint or tarragon.
> – Add a finely chopped onion and 4 chopped cherry tomatoes.

■ INGREDIENTS

- 8 large zucchini
  (courgettes)
- 7 oz (200 g) finely ground
  lean pork
- 1 Italian pork sausage,
  peeled and crumbled
- 3½ oz (100 g) mortadella
  (or ham), coarsely chopped
- ½ cup (2 oz/60 g)
  Parmesan cheese, freshly
  grated
- 2 tablespoons parsley,
  3 cloves garlic, finely
  chopped
- 2 eggs, beaten
- salt and freshly ground
  black pepper
- ½ cup (4 fl oz/125 ml)
  oil, for frying
- 4 tablespoons extra-virgin
  olive oil
- 1⅔ lb (800 g) tomatoes,
  peeled and chopped
- 6 basil leaves, torn

*Wine: a dry red
(Barbera d'Asti)*

■ INGREDIENTS

- 2 cloves garlic
- 2 tablespoons extra-virgin olive oil
- 2 tablespoons butter
- 1¾ lb small zucchini
  (courgettes), cut into
  wheels
- salt and freshly ground
  black pepper
- 3 tablespoons parsley,
  finely chopped

Wine: a dry red (Chianti)

Right:
Zucchine trifolate

Peperoni ripieni in tegame
Stuffed bell peppers

Serves: 4; Preparation: 20 minutes; Cooking: 35 minutes; Level of difficulty: Simple

Trim the stalks of the bell peppers to about 1 in (2.5 cm). Cut their tops off about ½ in (1 cm) from the top and set aside. Remove the core and seeds. § Soak the bread in cold water for 10 minutes. Squeeze out excess moisture, crumble, and place in a bowl. Season with salt and pepper. § Add the capers, olives, garlic, parsley, basil, anchovies, tomatoes, Parmesan, and Provolone. Pour in the vinegar and half the oil and mix thoroughly. § Stuff the bell peppers with the filling, replace the tops, and stand them upright in a pan that is at least as tall as they are. Add the remaining oil and ½ cup (4 fl oz/125 ml) of water. § Partially cover the pan and cook over medium-high heat. § Baste the bell peppers with liquid from the bottom of the pan from time to time. § After about 20 minutes pierce a bell pepper with the point of a sharp knife; if it penetrates easily, remove the lid and let some of the moisture evaporate. When done, the bell peppers will be soft and well-cooked. § Serve hot. The delicious dark stock can be poured over the bell peppers or served separately. § This dish makes a perfect entrée, or the main course in a light lunch.

Fiori e zucchine all'olio
Potatoes and zucchini with zucchini flowers

An eyecatching and distinctly southern Italian dish, from the Campania region around Naples. The original recipe calls for fresh chilies; add 2 for a mild dish and 4 for a spicy dish. If you can't get fresh chilies, use the crushed dried variety. Add the chilies together with the zucchini.

Serves: 4; Preparation: 15 minutes; Cooking: 25 minutes; Level of difficulty: Simple

Sauté the garlic with the oil in a skillet (frying pan) until light gold. § Add the potatoes, cover, and simmer for 15 minutes, stirring frequently. § Add the zucchini and season with salt, pepper, and mint. Simmer, partially covered, for 5 minutes more. If the vegetables are too watery, remove the lid and let some of the moisture evaporate. § Trim the stems of the zucchini flowers just below the bloom, wash carefully, and pat dry with paper towels. § Add 15 flowers to the zucchini and potatoes and cook for 5 minutes more, or until the vegetables are soft but not mushy. § Transfer to a heated serving dish, garnish with the remaining zucchini flowers, and serve hot.

■ INGREDIENTS

- 4 large red or yellow bell peppers (capsicums)
- 8 slices day-old bread
- salt and freshly ground black pepper
- 1 cup (3½ oz/100 g) capers
- 2 cups (7 oz/100 g) black olives, coarsely chopped
- 3 cloves garlic, 3 tablespoons parsley, finely chopped
- 12 fresh basil leaves
- 8 anchovy fillets, crumbled
- 12 oz (350 g) tomatoes, peeled and chopped
- 1½ cups (6 oz/180 g) Parmesan, freshly grated
- 1 cup (4 oz/125 g) Provolone cheese, freshly grated
- 1 tablespoon white wine vinegar
- ½ cup (4 fl oz/125 ml) extra-virgin olive oil

Wine: a dry red (Chianti Classico)

■ INGREDIENTS

- 2 cloves garlic, finely chopped
- 4 tablespoons extra-virgin olive oil
- 8 small new potatoes
- 6 medium zucchini (courgettes), cut in thick wheels
- salt and freshly ground black pepper
- 2 tablespoons mint, finely chopped
- 20 zucchini (courgette) flowers

Wine: a dry rosé (Ravello)

Right:
Fagioli all'uccelletto

■ INGREDIENTS

- 4 cloves garlic, minced
- ⅓ cup (3½ fl oz/100 ml) extra-virgin olive oil
- 14 oz (450 g) tomatoes, peeled and chopped
- 8 leaves fresh sage
- salt and pepper
- 2¼ cups (8½ oz/250 g) white kidney beans, canned, or soaked and pre-cooked

Wine: a dry red (Chianti Classico)

FAGIOLI ALL'UCCELLETTO
Tuscan-style kidney beans

*This is an old Florentine favorite. It is delicious when cooked in an earthenware pot.
For a spicier dish, add ½ teaspoon crushed chilies.*

Serves: 4; Preparation: 10 minutes; Cooking: 25 minutes; Level of difficulty: Simple

Sauté the garlic in the oil and as soon as it turns golden, add the tomatoes, sage, salt, and pepper. § Simmer over medium heat for 10 minutes. § As the sauce starts to thicken, add the beans and cook for about 15 more minutes. § Serve hot directly from the pot.

Peperoni vivaci
Mixed bell peppers with garlic and capers

Serves: 4; Preparation: 15 minutes; Cooking: 20-25 minutes; Level of difficulty: Simple

Cut the bell peppers lengthwise into ½-in (1-cm) strips. § Sauté the garlic with the oil in a large skillet (frying pan). Add the bell peppers and press them down with the lid. Season with salt. § Cook over medium heat for about 15 minutes, or until the strips start to wilt. Stir from time to time with a wooden fork. § When the bell peppers are tender, turn the heat up to high and pour the vinegar and capers over the top. Mix rapidly, and cook for 2–3 minutes more to let the vinegar evaporate. § Serve hot or at room temperature.

VARIATION
– Add 4 crumbled anchovy fillets with the vinegar and capers. In this case, use less salt.

■ INGREDIENTS

- 2 red, 1 yellow, 1 green medium bell peppers (capsicums)
- 3 cloves garlic, finely chopped
- 4 tablespoons extra-virgin olive oil
- salt
- ⅓ cup (3½ fl oz/100 ml) red wine vinegar
- 2 tablespoons capers

Wine: a young dry red (Chianti Novello)

Peperonata
Mixed bell peppers

*One of the classic Italian vegetable dishes.
It is particularly tasty when cooked in an earthenware pot.*

Serves: 4; Preparation: 20 minutes; Cooking: 30 minutes; Level of difficulty: Simple

Place the vegetables in a large, heavy-bottomed saucepan or earthenware pot. Add the oil, garlic, basil, salt, and pepper. Cover and cook over medium heat. § After 15 minutes turn the heat up to medium-high and partially uncover to let some of the liquid from the bell peppers evaporate. § As the dish cooks, the potatoes will soften, absorbing the flavors of the other vegetables. § Traditionally served as a side dish with boiled or roasted meats, *Peperonata* is also good on its own with rice, couscous, or baked potatoes.

VARIATION
– For a stronger, more distinctive flavor, add 1 medium diced eggplant (aubergine), black olives, and a sprinkling of oregano.

■ INGREDIENTS

- 4 bell peppers (capsicums), mixed red, yellow and green, cut in ½-in (1-cm) strips
- 3 onions, thickly sliced
- 1 lb (500 g) tomatoes, peeled and chopped
- 3 medium potatoes, cut in 1-in (2.5 cm) squares
- ⅓ cup (3½ fl oz/100 ml) extra-virgin olive oil
- 3 cloves garlic, finely chopped
- 8 fresh basil leaves, torn
- salt and freshly ground black pepper

Wine: a dry red (Sangiovese di Romagna)

Right: *Peperoni vivaci*

Fagiolini in umido con carote

Green beans and carrots cooked with onions, garlic, and tomatoes

Serves: 4; Preparation: 15 minutes; Cooking: 30 minutes; Level of difficulty: Simple

Put all the ingredients in a large, heavy-bottomed pan (or earthenware pot). Season with salt and pepper. § Cover and cook for 20 minutes over medium heat, stirring frequently. At first the beans will stay on top until the steam softens them and you can mix them in. § Uncover the pan and continue cooking until the sauce has reduced and the beans are crunchy but cooked. § Serve hot or at room temperature as a side dish for boiled or sautéed meats, or with rice, potatoes, or fresh bread as a light lunch.

VARIATION
— Add 2 large stalks of diced celery.

Cipolline brasate al vino

Baby onions braised in white wine

Serves: 4; Preparation: 10 minutes; Cooking: 30 minutes; Level of difficulty: Simple

Place the onions, oil, and butter in sautè pan. Sauté over high heat for about 10 minutes, stirring the onions with a wooden spoon until evenly browned. Season with salt and pepper. § Add the wine and bay leaves, partially cover, and cook for 15 more minutes. § Uncover and let the sauce thicken. § Serve hot or cold with any kind of roast meat or fish.

VARIATIONS
— Add 1 tablespoon of tomato paste with the wine, to make the onions pink.
— For a sweeter, more aromatic dish, soak 2 tablespoons of raisins in the wine. Add the raisins and a bouquet of herbs (thyme, marjoram, mint) together with the bay leaves.

Melanzane al funghetto
Eggplant cooked in tomato and garlic

This dish also makes an excellent pasta sauce. For 4 people, add 3 extra tomatoes and another tablespoon of oil to the ingredients listed here. Serve with 1 lb (500 g) of any sort of dried short pasta (penne, conchiglie, fusilli, macaroni) cooked in salted, boiling water until al dente.

Serves: 4; Preparation: 15 minutes; Cooking: 30 minutes; Level of difficulty: Simple

Trim the ends off the eggplants and cut them in quarters lengthwise. Slice the quarters into pieces about 1 in (2.5 cm) long. § Sauté the garlic in the oil in a large skillet (frying pan) until it turns gold. § Add the eggplant, season with salt and pepper, stir well and cover. Cook over medium-low heat for 15 minutes. § Add the tomatoes, mix well, and cook for 10 more minutes over medium heat. § For the last 5 minutes, remove the lid and add the herbs. § Serve hot as a pasta sauce, or as a side dish with roast or fried meat or fish.

■ INGREDIENTS

- 6 long eggplants (aubergines)
- 4 cloves garlic, finely chopped
- 3 tablespoons extra-virgin olive oil
- salt and freshly ground black pepper
- 3 medium tomatoes, peeled and chopped
- 2 tablespoons parsley, finely chopped

Wine: a dry red (Valpolicella)

Melanzane a librino
Filled eggplant "sandwiches"

Serves: 4; Preparation: 2¼ hours; Cooking: 30 minutes; Level of difficulty: Medium

Using a sharp knife, cut each eggplant in three crosswise. Slice each piece down the middle, leaving it attached on one side, and open it out like a book. § Place the eggplants in layers in a large dish, and sprinkle with salt. Cover with a plate with a heavy weight on top to press the bitter liquid out of the eggplants. Leave to degorge for 2 hours. § Beat the eggs in a bowl until foamy, add the pork, parsley, garlic, and Parmesan. Blend well with a fork for 2–3 minutes. § Put the eggplants in a colander and rinse well under cold running water to remove all the salt. Squeeze the moisture out gently with your hands and pat dry with paper towels. § Using a teaspoon, stuff the pieces of eggplant with the filling so that they look like plump little sandwiches. § Heat the frying oil in a skillet and dip the eggplant sandwiches in one by one, turning them with two forks to seal the edges so that the filling stays inside. § Drain on paper towels. § Heat the olive oil in a sauté pan and add the tomatoes and basil. Cook over medium heat for 15 minutes. Season with salt and pepper. § Add the eggplant sandwiches and cover with sauce. Simmer over low heat for 10 minutes, or until the sauce begins to reduce. § Serve hot with a green salad as a main course.

■ INGREDIENTS

- 8 long eggplants (aubergines)
- salt
- 4 eggs
- 1 lb (500 g) ground pork
- 2 tablespoons parsley, finely chopped
- 3 cloves garlic, finely chopped
- ¾ cup Parmesan cheese, freshly grated
- oil for frying
- 1¼ lb (600 g) tomatoes, peeled and chopped
- 6 leaves fresh basil
- 4 tablespoons extra-virgin olive oil
- freshly ground black pepper

Wine: a dry red (Brindisi Riserva)

Right:
Melanzane al funghetto

Carciofi Ritti

Roman-style stuffed braised artichokes

This dish is also known as "Carciofi alla Romana" because it come from Lazio, the region around Rome.

Serves: 4; Preparation: 30 minutes; Cooking: 25-30 minutes; Level of difficulty: Simple

Clean the artichokes by trimming the tops and removing the tough outer leaves. Cut the stems very short so that the artichokes can stand upright. Place in a bowl of cold water with the lemon juice. Set aside for 10 minutes. § Place the artichokes in a sauté pan just large enough to hold them. They should stand upright. Add 2 tablespoons of oil. § Open the leaves carefully and stuff with garlic and parsley (leave 2 spoonfuls for garnishing), pancetta, Pecorino, and Parmesan. Press the filling down and close the leaves. § Sprinkle the stuffed artichokes with the remaining garlic and parsley and pour the wine and remaining oil over the top. Season with salt (not too much–the pancetta and Pecorino are both salty) and pepper. § Cover with foil, leaving a small opening for the steam, and cook over medium heat. § Baste the artichokes with their sauce from time to time during cooking. When the sauce has reduced to about 1 inch in the bottom of the pan, the artichokes are ready. § Serve hot as a light lunch, or as a side dish with roast or grilled meat.

> Variation
> – The artichokes can also be filled as follows: crumble about 7 oz (200 g) of Mozzarella cheese in a bowl with 2 tablespoons of finely chopped parsley, 3 tablespoons of bread crumbs, 3 tablespoons of freshly grated Parmesan cheese, and 2 beaten eggs. Season with salt and pepper, mix well, and stuff the artichokes. Cook with wine and oil as above. This recipe gives the artichokes a more delicate flavor.

■ INGREDIENTS

- 8 large artichokes
- juice of 1 lemon
- ⅓ cup (3½ fl oz/100 ml) extra-virgin olive oil
- 4 cloves garlic, 4 tablespoons parsley, finely chopped together
- 2 cups (8 oz/250 g) pancetta, diced
- 5 oz (150 g) Pecorino romano cheese, flaked
- ½ cup (2 oz/60 g) Parmesan cheese, freshly grated
- 1¼ cups (10 fl oz/300 ml) dry white wine
- salt and freshly ground black pepper

Wine: a rosé
(Lagrein Rosato)

Spezzatino di Carciofi

Artichoke stew

Serves: 4; Preparation: 20 minutes; Cooking: 25 minutes; Level of difficulty: Simple

Clean the artichokes as described above. Remove all but the tender, white inner leaves. Peel the stems and cut them into wheels. § Put the artichokes and stems in a bowl of cold water with the lemon juice for 10 minutes. § Drain the artichokes and cut them into quarters. § Place the artichoke quarters and stems, garlic, oil, wine, salt, and pepper in a

■ INGREDIENTS

- 8 medium artichokes
- juice of 1 lemon
- 3 cloves garlic, finely chopped
- 4 tablespoons extra-virgin olive oil
- 1 cup (8 fl oz/250 ml) dry white wine

Right:
Spezzatino di carciofi

- salt and freshly ground black pepper
- 3 tablespoons parsley, finely chopped

Wine: a dry white (Greco di Tufo)

heavy-bottomed pan. Cook for 20 minutes covered, then uncover and add the parsley; stir and finish cooking without a lid. § Serve hot at lunch with a platter of fresh, light cheeses (Mozzarella, Ricotta, Caprino). The artichokes can also be served as a side dish for liver cooked in butter and sage, or with oven-roasted or braised meats.

VARIATION
– Replace the parsley with mint or calamint and add 1½ tablespoons of tomato paste to the cooking liquid.

Mamme di carciofi ripiene
Stuffed artichokes

■ INGREDIENTS

Serves: 4; Preparation: 20 minutes; Cooking: 1 hour; Level of difficulty: Medium

Clean the artichokes as described on page 6. Trim the stems short so that the artichokes will stand upright in the pot. Chop the stems coarsely and soak them with the artichokes in a bowl of cold water and lemon juice for 10 minutes. § Beat the eggs in a bowl until foamy. Season with salt and pepper. § Add the pork, sausage, prosciutto, Parmesan, garlic, parsley, salt, and pepper and blend well with a fork. § Using a teaspoon, fill the heart of each artichoke. § Heat the frying oil in a skillet (frying pan) and when it is hot enough hold each artichoke upside down in the oil for about 2 minutes, to seal in the filling. Roll the artichokes in the oil for 2 more minutes to cook the leaves. Using two forks, remove from the oil and set aside. § Place the olive oil, tomatoes, basil, artichoke stems, salt, and pepper in a sauté pan and simmer over medium heat for 10 minutes. § Add the stuffed artichokes and baste them with the sauce. Cover and simmer for 20 minutes. Uncover and cook for 10 more minutes, or until the sauce has reduced. § Serve hot.

- 8 large artichokes
- juice of 1 lemon
- 4 eggs
- salt and freshly ground black pepper
- 5 oz (150 g) ground lean pork
- 1 Italian pork sausage, skinned and crumbled
- 1½ cups (12 oz/350 g) chopped prosciutto
- 1½ cups (6 oz/180 g) Parmesan cheese, freshly grated
- 3 cloves garlic, 2 tablespoons parsley, finely chopped
- 1 cup (8 fl oz/250 ml) oil, for frying
- ½ cup (4 fl oz/125 ml) extra-virgin olive oil
- 1½ lb (750 g) tomatoes, peeled and chopped
- 10 fresh basil leaves

Wine: a dry red (Sassicaia)

Tortino di carciofi
Florentine artichoke omelet

■ INGREDIENTS

A classic Florentine recipe, as old as the city itself. A real Florentine artichoke omelet should be slightly underdone; the eggs should be cooked underneath and moist on top.

Serves: 4; Preparation: 20 minutes; Cooking: 25-30 minutes; Level of difficulty: Simple

Clean the artichokes as described on page 6. Cut the stems short. Soak in a bowl of cold water and lemon juice for 10 minutes. § Cut the artichokes into ½-in slices and put them in a large skillet (frying pan) with the oil. Add the water and salt to taste, cover and cook for 7–8 minutes. § Uncover and continue cooking until the artichokes are tender and the water has evaporated. § Beat the eggs with salt and pepper until foamy and pour over the artichokes. Cover and cook for 5 minutes over medium heat. Uncover and continue cooking. As the egg begins to set, stir carefully so that it cooks evenly. § Serve hot with a green salad.

- 5 large artichokes
- juice of 1 lemon
- 4 tablespoons extra-virgin olive oil
- 5 eggs
- ½ cup (4 fl oz/125 ml) water
- salt and freshly ground black pepper

Wine: a dry red (Chianti)

Right:
Tortino di carciofi

■ INGREDIENTS

- 3 large heads escarole
- 4 tablespoons extra-virgin olive oil
- ⅓ cup (2 oz/60 g) pine nuts
- ⅓ cup (2 oz/60 g) raisins, soaked for 30 minutes in water
- 12 pitted and chopped black olives
- salt and freshly ground black pepper
- ⅓ cup (1½ oz/50 g) capers
- 4 anchovy fillets, finely chopped, or 3 curls of anchovy paste

Wine: a dry white
(Pinot Grigio)

INDIVIA SCAROLA DOLCE FORTE DELICATA

Escarole with pine nuts, capers, olives, raisins, and anchovies

Serves: 4; Preparation: 10 minutes; Cooking: 25 minutes; Level of difficulty: Simple

Use the green leaves of the escarole and set the creamy white hearts aside to use in a salad. § Blanch the leaves in salted, boiling water, drain well, and spread in a colander to dry for about 10 minutes. § Heat the oil in a sauté pan and add the escarole, pine nuts, raisins, olives, salt, and pepper. Sauté over medium heat for 10 minutes. Toss the leaves from time to time as they cook. § Add the capers and anchovy, toss well and cook until any excess water has evaporated. § Serve hot as an entrée, or as a side dish with roast or barbecued meat – the earthy flavor is perfect with both white and red meats.

■ INGREDIENTS

- 2 large heads celery
- juice of 1 lemon
- salt and freshly ground black pepper
- 4 tablespoons extra-virgin olive oil
- 1 large potato, diced
- ½ cup (2 oz/60 g) pancetta, diced
- 1 cup (8 fl oz/250 ml) fresh cream

Wine: a young dry red
(Vino Novello)

CUORI DI SEDANO DELICATI

Celery hearts in cream sauce with pancetta and potato

Serves: 4; Preparation: 5 minutes; Cooking: 30 minutes; Level of difficulty: Simple

Remove the tough outer stalks of celery and cut the ends off level with the hearts. Divide the inner stalks in half lengthwise. § Bring a pot of salted water with the lemon juice to a boil and cook the celery for 7–8 minutes. Drain well and place on a serving dish. § Heat the oil in a skillet (frying pan) and fry the potato until tender. § Remove most of the oil and cook the pancetta until crisp. § Heat the cream in a saucepan with salt and pepper to taste. Cook until it reduces. § Pour the cream over the celery hearts, and sprinkle the potatoes and pancetta on top. § Serve hot as an appetizer, or as side dish with braised white meats.

Left:
Cuori di sedano delicati

VARIATION
– For a tastier dish, add 2 tablespoons of sharp, grated cheese to the cream before heating it (Pecorino romano or Provolone) or Parmesan cheese with a tablespoon of *Basic tomato sauce* (see recipe p. 16).

Cavolini di Bruxelles alla diavola
Hot and spicy Brussels sprouts

■ INGREDIENTS

- 2 lb (1 kg) Brussels sprouts
- 3 cloves garlic, finely chopped
- 3 tablespoons extra-virgin olive oil
- 1 cup (4 oz/125 g) smoked pancetta (or bacon), diced
- 1 Italian sausage, skinned and crumbled
- ½ teaspoon crushed chilies
- salt
- 1 bunch chives, coarsely chopped

Wine: a dry red (Sangiovese)

Serves: 4-6; Preparation: 10 minutes; Cooking: 25 minutes; Level of difficulty: Simple

Cook the Brussels sprouts in salted, boiling water for 7–8 minutes, drain well, and set aside. § In a large skillet (frying pan), sauté the garlic in the oil until pale gold. § Add the pancetta and sausage. Sauté briefly and stir in the Brussels sprouts and crushed chilies. § Season with salt, cover, and cook for 10 minutes. § Uncover, sprinkle with the chives and cook for 5 more minutes. § Serve piping hot on a bed of rice as a main course, or as a side dish with barbecued pork chops or veal roast.

Cavolini di Bruxelles al curry
Curried Brussels sprouts

■ INGREDIENTS

- 1 medium onion, finely chopped
- 2 tablespoons butter
- 1 tablespoon sifted all-purpose (plain) flour
- 2 cups (16 fl oz/500 ml) *Beef stock (see recipe p. 20)*
- 1 Golden Delicious apple, peeled and thinly sliced
- 1 cup (8 fl oz/250 ml) fresh cream
- 1½ tablespoons curry powder
- salt and freshly ground black pepper
- 2 lb (1 kg) Brussels sprouts

Wine: a dry white (Sauvignon)

Serves: 4-6; Preparation: 20 minutes; Cooking: 30 minutes; Level of difficulty: Simple

Sauté the onion in the butter in a large skillet until soft. § Add the flour and mix well, stirring rapidly with a wooden spoon. Add half the beef stock a little at a time, stirring constantly. § Add the apple and stir in the remaining stock a little at a time as the sauce simmers over low heat for about 20 minutes. The mixture should boil slowly as the apple disintegrates and blends in with the other ingredients. After 20 minutes the sauce should be thick and creamy. § Add the cream and curry powder, season with salt and pepper, and simmer for 5 more minutes, stirring constantly. § In the meantime, cook the Brussels sprouts for about 10 minutes in salted, boiling water. Drain well and arrange on a heated serving dish. § Pour the hot sauce over the top and serve immediately as a main course with saffron-flavored rice, or as a side dish with chicken cooked in a white wine sauce or veal scaloppini braised with onions.

Right: *Cavolini di Bruxelles al curry*

Funghi misti in fricassea
Mixed mushrooms in egg sauce

Timing is important in this recipe. The egg sauce must be poured over the mushrooms the moment they are removed from the heat and tossed quickly so that the egg cooks evenly.

Serves: 4; Preparation: 15 minutes; Cooking: 25 minutes; Level of difficulty: Medium

Sauté the onion in a large skillet (frying pan) with the oil. § Chop the larger mushrooms in thick slices and leave the smaller varieties whole. § Add the mushrooms to the skillet. Season with salt and pepper, cover, and cook for 15–20 minutes over medium-low heat. Stir frequently. § When the mushrooms are cooked, remove from heat and transfer to a heated serving dish. § While the mushrooms are cooking, beat the egg yolks in a bowl with the lemon juice and parsley until foamy. § Pour the egg sauce over the mushrooms and toss quickly so that the egg cooks evenly. § Serve with a large green salad and fresh bread as a light lunch.

■ INGREDIENTS

- 1 medium onion, finely chopped
- 4 tablespoons extra-virgin olive oil
- 2 lb (1 kg) mixed fresh or frozen mushrooms (porcini, white, chanterelle, or Caesar's), washed and trimmed
- salt and freshly ground black pepper
- 4 egg yolks
- juice of 1 lemon
- 2 tablespoons parsley, finely chopped

Wine: a young, dry red (Novello Falò)

Funghi porcini trifolati
Stewed porcini mushrooms

The traditional Italian recipe calls for fresh porcini mushrooms, which are hard to find outside Italy or France. If you can't get porcini mushrooms, replace them with the same quantity of fresh shiitake mushrooms, or with 1½ lb (750 g) of white mushrooms and ¼ cup of dried porcini mushrooms soaked in a bowl of warm water for 20 minutes.

Serves: 4-6; Preparation: 15 minutes; Cooking: 15 minutes; Level of difficulty: Simple

Trim the stalks of the mushrooms and separate the heads from the stems. § Cut the stems in half. Chop the stems and heads in thick slices. § Sauté the garlic in a large sauté pan until golden. Add the stems and sauté for 7–8 minutes. § Add the mushroom heads, salt, and pepper and stir carefully with a wooden spoon. § Add the calamint or thyme and finish cooking over low heat. § Serve hot as an appetizer on squares of toasted whole-wheat bread, or as a side dish with braised or stewed meat.

■ INGREDIENTS

- 2 lb (1 kg) fresh porcini mushrooms
- 3 large cloves garlic, finely chopped
- 4 tablespoons extra-virgin olive oil
- salt and freshly ground black pepper
- 1 tablespoon fresh, or ½ tablespoon dried, calamint or thyme

Wine: a dry red (Brunello di Montalcino)

VARIATION
– Replace the porcini with chanterelle mushrooms and add 3 cherry tomatoes (cut in half and squashed with a fork) halfway through cooking.

Right:
Funghi porcini trifolati

■ INGREDIENTS

- 2 lb (1 kg) white mushrooms
- 4 medium potatoes, diced
- ⅓ cup (3½ fl oz/100 ml) extra-virgin olive oil
- 3 cloves garlic, crushed
- salt and black pepper
- ⅔ cup (4 oz/125 g) pine nuts
- ½ cup (2 oz/60 g) almond shavings
- 2 tablespoons mint, finely chopped

Wine: a dry red (Teroldego)

Funghetti e patatine ai pinoli
Mushrooms and potatoes with pine nuts

Serves: 4; Preparation: 10 minutes; Cooking: 25 minutes; Level of difficulty: Simple

Chop any larger mushrooms in thick slices and leave the smaller ones whole. § Fry the potatoes with the oil and garlic in a large skillet (frying pan). § Add the mushrooms and sauté. Season with salt and pepper, cover, and cook for 5 minutes. § Uncover and let some of the moisture evaporate. Stir in the pine nuts and almonds and cook for 10 more minutes. § Sprinkle with mint just before removing from heat. § Serve hot as a main course or light lunch with a large mixed salad.

Pisellini primavera al prezzemolo e prosciutto
Spring peas with prosciutto and parsley

Serves: 4; Preparation: 15 minutes; Cooking: 25 minutes; Level of difficulty: Simple

Sauté the prosciutto in the oil in a large skillet (frying pan) for 5 minutes. Remove from heat. § Let the oil cool, then add the peas, garlic, parsley, and water. Partially cover and simmer for about 15 minutes. § Season with salt and pepper. § Serve hot as a side dish with roast beef or oven-baked fish.

VARIATIONS
— Replace the garlic with 1 medium onion, finely chopped.
— Add a teaspoon of sugar to make the peas sweeter.

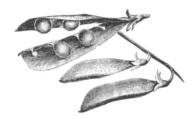

INGREDIENTS

- 1½ lb (750 g) fresh or frozen peas
- 4 tablespoons extra-virgin olive oil
- 1½ cups (12 oz/350 g) prosciutto, diced
- 2 large cloves garlic, finely chopped
- 1 cup (8 fl oz/250 ml) water
- 3 tablespoons parsley, finely chopped
- salt and freshly ground black pepper

*Wine: a dry red
(Chianti Classico)*

Mousse di piselli
Pea mousse

Serves: 4; Preparation: 2½ hours; Cooking: 15 minutes; Level of difficulty: Simple

Bring 2 quarts (4 pints/2 liters) of salted water to a boil in a pan and cook the peas and onion for 10–15 minutes. § Drain well and set aside to cool. § Place the Ricotta, peas, onion, and oil in a food processor and chop until the mixture is creamy. Season with salt and pepper. § Line a 1-quart (1-liter) pudding mold with plastic wrap and pour the mixture in, pressing with a spoon to eliminate any air bubbles. Knock the mold against the work bench to eliminate air pockets. § Refrigerate for at least 2 hours. § Invert onto a round serving dish and garnish with the carrot wheels and sprigs of parsley. § Serve on slices of whole-wheat toast as an appetizer or as a side dish with braised or roast fish.

VARIATION
— For a sharper flavor, replace the Ricotta with Robiola or Caprino cheese and place 2 cups (1 lb/500 g) of finely chopped lean ham in layers at the center of the mousse.

INGREDIENTS

- 1 lb (500 g) shelled or frozen peas
- 1 medium onion, cut in half
- 1½ cups (14 oz/450 g) Ricotta cheese
- 3 tablespoons extra-virgin olive oil
- salt and freshly ground black pepper
- 1 carrot, cut in very thin wheels
- 8 tiny sprigs parsley

*Wine: a dry red
(Cabernet)*

*Right: Pisellini primavera al
prezzemolo e prosciutto*

Asparagi eleganti
Asparagus with brandy and cream sauce

Serves: 4; Preparation: 15 minutes; Cooking: 25 minutes; Level of difficulty: Simple

Choose a pan large enough to lay the asparagus flat, fill with cold water, and bring to a boil. Add 1 tablespoon of salt and cook the asparagus for 7–10 minutes (depending on the thickness of the stalks). § Drain well and cut off the tough white part at the bottoms of the stalks. § Melt the butter in a skillet and add the asparagus. Season with salt and pepper and cook for 3–4 minutes over medium heat. § Pour in the brandy and let it evaporate. Keep the asparagus moving by shaking the skillet gently by the handle. § Meanwhile, put the cream and bread crumbs in a saucepan, mix well and cook over medium heat for 10–15 minutes, or until the sauce is thick and creamy. Stir frequently. § Place the asparagus stalks on a heated serving dish and pour the sauce over the top. § Serve hot as an entrée.

■ INGREDIENTS

- 2 lb (1 kg) fresh asparagus
- salt and freshly ground black pepper
- 4 tablespoons butter
- ⅓ cup (3½ fl oz/100 ml) brandy
- 2⅓ cups (20 fl oz/ 600 ml) heavy (double) cream
- 1 tablespoon bread crumbs

Wine: a dry white (Corvo Bianco)

Cicoria catalogna in padella
Spicy chicory with garlic and anchovies

Serves: 4; Preparation: 10 minutes; Cooking: 30 minutes; Level of difficulty: Simple

Trim the head of chicory, remove any yellow or wilted leaves and divide it in two. Wash in cold running water. § Cook in a pan of salted, boiling water for 10–15 minutes. § Drain thoroughly without squeezing and cut lengthwise into 1-in (2.5-cm) pieces. § Sauté the garlic in the oil in a large skillet until golden. § Add the chicory and chilies, and season with a dash of salt (not too much—remember the capers and anchovies to be added later). § Cook over medium heat for about 10 minutes, stirring frequently. § Stir the anchovies and capers in over high heat for 2–3 minutes. § Serve on a heated serving dish with beef sautéed in sage and garlic, broiled sausages, or mixed roast meats.

■ INGREDIENTS

- 1 large head chicory
- 5 cloves garlic, finely chopped
- ½ teaspoon crushed chilies
- ⅓ cup (3½ fl oz/100 ml) extra-virgin olive oil
- salt
- 8 anchovy fillets, crumbled
- ⅓ cup (1¾ oz/50 g) capers

Wine: a dry red (Valpolicella)

Right:
Asparagi eleganti

■ INGREDIENTS

- 2 lb (1 kg) fresh or frozen spinach
- 4 large cloves garlic, finely chopped
- 4 tablespoons extra-virgin olive oil
- salt

Wine: a dry white
(Riesling Italico)

SPINACI SALTATI

Spinach sautéed with olive oil and garlic

Serves: 6; Preparation: 10 minutes; Cooking: 30 minutes; Level of difficulty: Simple

Cook the spinach in a pot of salted, boiling water until tender (3–4 minutes if frozen, 8–10 minutes if fresh). Drain, cool under cold running water, squeeze out excess moisture, and chop coarsely. § Sauté the garlic in the oil until golden. § Add the spinach and cook over medium-high heat for 3–4 minutes, tossing continually, so that the spinach absorbs the flavors of the garlic and oil. § Serve hot with poached eggs and *Basic tomato sauce* (see recipe page 16), or as a side dish with roast or braised meat.

Cardi al sugo di carne e parmigiano
Cardoons in meat sauce with Parmesan cheese

A cardoon looks a bit like a large white celery. It is closely related to the artichoke, although it has a much stronger taste. Cardoons are not always easy to find, even in Italy. For a completely different, but equally delicious dish, replace the cardoon with the same amount of celery. In this case, there is no need to soak the celery in lemon juice, and cooking time will be reduced to 15–20 minutes.

Serves: 4; Preparation: 15 minutes; Cooking: 35 minutes; Level of difficulty: Simple

Prepare the cardoon by removing any damaged outer stalks and tough filaments with a sharp knife. Separate the stalks from the heart and cut them into pieces about 3 in (8 cm) long. Wash well and soak in a bowl of cold water with the lemon juice for about 10 minutes. § Bring a pot of salted water to a boil. Add the flour and pieces of cardoon and cook for 20 minutes. Drain well. § Heat the meat sauce with the butter in a large sauté pan. Add the cardoon pieces a few at a time and mix well with the sauce. When they are all in the pan, season with salt and pepper. Partially cover, and cook over low heat for 10–15 minutes, or until the cardoons are tender. Stir frequently. § When cooked, sprinkle with Parmesan and let stand for a minute, covered. § Serve hot at lunch with fresh bread and a green or mixed salad.

■ INGREDIENTS

- 1 cardoon, about 2 lb (1 kg)
- juice of 2 lemons
- 1½ tablespoons all-purpose (plain) flour
- ¼ cup (2 oz/60 g) butter
- ½ quantity *Meat sauce* (see recipe p. 16)
- salt and freshly ground black pepper
- 4 tablespoons Parmesan cheese, freshly grated

Wine: a dry red
(Rosso di Montepulciano)

Carote caramellate al prezzemolo
Carrots in caramel sauce with parsley

If the sauce reduces too much during cooking, sprinkle with white wine (before adding the parsley).

Serves: 6; Preparation: 10 minutes; Cooking: 25 minutes; Level of difficulty: Simple

Peel the carrots with a peeler or scrape them with a knife. Rinse well under cold running water. § Cut the carrots into sticks about 2 in (5 cm) long (if you are using baby carrots, leave them whole). § Place in a large sauté pan and almost cover with cold water. Add half the butter cut into cubes. § Cook over high heat until the water evaporates. § Season with salt and pepper, add the remaining butter, and sprinkle with the sugar. Sauté the carrots until they are all a bright orange color, shiny and caramel-coated. § Add the parsley, mix well, and serve hot with braised or roasted fish or meat.

■ INGREDIENTS

- 3 lb (1½ kg) carrots
- ½ cup (4 oz/125 g) butter
- salt and freshly ground black pepper
- 2 tablespoons sugar
- 3 tablespoons parsley, finely chopped

Wine: a dry white
(Orvieto Classico),

Right:
Carote caramellate al prezzemolo

■ INGREDIENTS

- 3 lb (1½ kg) fava beans (broad beans), in their pods
- ⅔ cup (3 oz/90 g) pancetta, diced
- 2 tablespoons extra-virgin olive oil
- 1 medium onion, finely chopped
- 1 cup (8 fl oz/250 ml) *Beef stock* (see recipe p. 20)
- salt and freshly ground black pepper

Wine: a dry white (Vernaccia di San Gimignano)

■ INGREDIENTS

- 1½ cups (6 oz/180 g) lentils, soaked in cold water overnight
- 1 medium onion, 1 large carrot, 2 stalks celery, all finely chopped together
- ½ cup (4 fl oz/125 ml) extra-virgin olive oil
- ½ cup (2 oz/60 g) diced pancetta
- 1 cup (8 fl oz/250 g) white wine
- 1½ tablespoons tomato paste, diluted in 2 tablespoons hot water
- 1 beef stock cube
- salt and freshly ground black pepper
- 5 Italian sausages, pricked with a fork so that excess fat is eliminated while frying

Wine: a dry red (Merlot)

Left: *Lenticchie stufate con salsiccia*

FAVE FRESCHE ALLA PANCETTA
Fresh fava beans with pancetta

Serves: 4; Preparation: 30 minutes; Cooking: 30 minutes; Level of difficulty: Simple

Pod the beans and set them aside in a bowl of cold water. § Put the pancetta and onion in a sauté pan with the oil and sauté over medium-low heat until the onion is light gold in color. § Drain the fava beans and add with the stock to the sauté pan. Season with salt and pepper. § Cover, and cook over medium-low heat for 20 minutes, or until the beans are tender and the stock has reduced. § Serve hot as an entrée.

LENTICCHIE STUFATE CON SALSICCIA
Stewed lentils with Italian sausages

Serves: 4; Preparation: 10 minutes; Cooking: 1½ hours; Level of difficulty: Simple

Discard any lentils floating on top of the water. § Put the lentils in a pot with just enough cold water to cover them. Season with salt. Simmer for 30 minutes, then drain. § Put the onion, carrot, celery, and pancetta in a large sauté pan with the oil and sauté until golden brown. § Add the lentils and stir for 2–3 minutes to mix them in well. § Pour in the white wine and let it evaporate a little, then add the diluted tomato paste and the stock cube. Season with salt and pepper, and cover with hot water. Cook for 40 minutes over low heat. § In the meantime, brown the sausages in a skillet (frying pan) with 2 tablespoons of cold water. Drain the excess fat and add the sausages to the lentils when they have been cooking for about 20 minutes, so they add their flavor to the dish. § When cooked, the lentils should be tender and the stew slightly liquid. If it is too watery, stir over high heat until it reduces sufficiently. § Serve hot as a hearty and complete main course.

VARIATION
– For a spicier dish, add 1 teaspoon crushed chilies with the tomato paste.

Involtini di verza
Stuffed cabbage rolls

Serves: 4; Preparation: 50 minutes; Cooking: 45 minutes; Level of difficulty: Medium

Trim the cabbage, discarding the tough outer leaves. Choose 8 large cabbage leaves, make a small cut in the stem of each and blanch them in salted, boiling water for 4–5 minutes. Drain well, and lay them to dry on a clean dish towel. § Put the beef, pork, sausages, Parmesan, eggs, garlic, parsley, salt, and pepper in a bowl and mix well with a fork. § Distribute the filling evenly, placing a part on one half of each leaf. Fold the other half over the top, press down, and tuck in the two remaining open ends. Tie with kitchen string. § Sauté the onion in the butter and oil in a large skillet until light gold. § Add the stuffed cabbage leaves. Cook on both sides, turning them carefully with a fork or spoon. § Add the tomatoes, season with salt and pepper and cook over medium-low heat for about 40 minutes. If the sauce becomes too dry, add the beef stock. § Serve hot as a main course with saffron risotto or plain white rice.

■ INGREDIENTS

- 1 medium cabbage
- 5 oz (150 g) lean ground beef
- 5 oz (150 g) lean ground pork
- 5 oz (150 g) Italian sausage, skinned and crumbled
- ½ cup (2 oz/60 g) Parmesan cheese, freshly grated
- 2 eggs
- 2 cloves garlic, 2 tablespoons parsley, finely chopped
- salt and pepper
- 2 tablespoons butter
- 3 tablespoons extra-virgin olive oil
- 1 onion, finely chopped
- 1¼ lb (600 g) tomatoes, peeled and chopped
- 1 cup *Beef stock* (see recipe p. 20)

Wine: a dry red (Bonarda)

Involtini di lattuga saporiti
Stuffed lettuce-leaf rolls

Serves: 4; Preparation: 30 minutes; Cooking: 40 minutes; Level of difficulty: Medium

Wash the lettuce leaves, taking care not to tear them. § Bring a pot of salted water to a boil and blanch each leaf by dipping it into the water for about 20 seconds. Lay the leaves on a clean dish towel to dry. § Brown the sausages in a skillet (frying pan) without oil. Add the wine and let it evaporate. Remove from heat and set to cool on a plate, leaving any fat in the skillet. § Beat the eggs in a bowl, add the salt, pepper, Edam, Parmesan, bread crumbs, and sausage. Mix well to make a smooth filling. § Distribute the filling evenly among the lettuce leaves and roll them up, folding in the ends to make packages or rolls. Tie with kitchen string. § Put the onion in a skillet with the oil over medium heat and sauté until soft. § Place the stuffed lettuce leaves in the skillet with the onion, cover, and cook for 5 minutes. Turn the lettuce rolls with a fork, uncover and cook for 5 more minutes. § Serve hot as a main course with mushroom risotto.

■ INGREDIENTS

- 8 large lettuce leaves
- 8 oz (250 g) Italian sausage, skinned and crumbled
- ¾ cup (7 fl oz/200 ml) dry white wine
- 2 eggs
- salt and black pepper
- 4 oz (125 g) Edam cheese, freshly grated
- 1 cup (4 oz/125 g) Parmesan cheese, freshly grated
- 3 tablespoons bread crumbs
- 4 tablespoons extra-virgin olive oil
- 1 medium onion, finely chopped

Wine: a dry white (Chardonnay)

Right: *Involtini di verza*

Baked Vegetables

A wide variety of vegetables can be baked to create pies, crêpes, molds, filled, or gratin dishes. They can be served hot as entrées, main courses, or light lunches, or let cool and presented as healthy after-school treats for hungry children or delicious snacks for the whole family.

Sformato di cavolfiore con olive
Cauliflower mold with black olives

Serves: 4; Preparation: 25 minutes; Cooking: 55 minutes; Level of difficulty: Simple

Divide the cauliflower into large florets and trim the stems. Cook in a pot of salted, boiling water for 5–7 minutes. Drain and set aside. § Prepare the béchamel sauce. § Chop the cauliflower with a heavy knife or in a food processor. § Combine the purée with the béchamel, Parmesan, olives, eggs, salt, pepper, and nutmeg. § Grease a ring mold about 10 in (25 cm) in diameter with a little butter and sprinkle with bread crumbs. Pour the mixture into the mold and place the mold in a larger container filled with water. § Cook in a preheated oven at 350°F/180°C/gas 4 for 45 minutes. § Invert the mold onto a platter while still hot. Serve hot or at room temperature.

Sformato di spinaci
Spinach mold

Like all the molds in this chapter, Sformato di spinaci *can be served as an entrée or main course, or as a side dish with meat or fish. Add a touch of color to this spinach mold by serving it with 1 quantity of* Basic tomato sauce, *well-reduced (see recipe p. 16).*

Serves: 4; Preparation: 30 minutes; Cooking: 1 hour; Level of difficulty: Medium

Cook the spinach in a pot of salted, boiling water until tender (3–4 minutes if frozen, 8–10 minutes if fresh). Drain, cool under cold running water, and squeeze out excess moisture. Chop with a heavy knife or in a food processor. § Put the spinach in a saucepan with the cream and stir over medium heat until all the moisture has been absorbed. Remove from heat. § Prepare the béchamel sauce. Set aside to cool for 5 minutes. § Combine the béchamel with the spinach purée and add the Parmesan, nutmeg, and egg yolks. Season with salt and pepper. § Beat the egg whites until stiff and carefully fold them into the spinach mixture. § Grease a ring mold about 10 in (25 cm) in diameter with a little butter and dust with flour. Pour the mixture into the mold. § Place the mold in a larger container filled with water and cook in a preheated oven at 350°F/180°C/gas 4 for 45 minutes. § Invert onto a platter while still hot. Serve hot or at room temperature.

■ INGREDIENTS

- 2 lb (1 kg) cauliflower head
- 1 quantity *Béchamel sauce* (see recipe p. 22)
- salt and freshly ground black pepper
- ¼ teaspoon nutmeg
- ½ cup (2 oz/60 g) Parmesan cheese, freshly grated
- 20 black olives, pitted and chopped
- 3 eggs, beaten until foamy
- butter to grease the mold and bread crumbs

Wine: a dry white (Melissa)

■ INGREDIENTS

- 1½ lb (750 g) fresh or frozen spinach
- salt and freshly ground black pepper
- 4 tablespoons heavy (double) cream
- 1 quantity *Béchamel sauce* (see recipe p. 22)
- ½ cup (2 oz/60 g) Parmesan cheese, freshly grated
- ¼ teaspoon nutmeg
- 2 eggs, separated
- butter and flour to grease and dust the mold

Wine: a dry white (Pinot Grigio)

Right: *Sformato di spinaci con salsa di pomodoro*

Sformato di zucchine con carote
Zucchini and carrot mold

Serves: 4-6; Preparation: 40 minutes; Cooking: 1½ hours; Level of difficulty: Medium

Put one-fifth of the zucchini in a skillet with 1 tablespoon of oil. Cook over medium heat for 5 minutes. Set aside. § Sauté the carrots and onions in the remaining oil for 5 minutes. § Add the remaining zucchini, partially cover, and cook for 10–15 minutes, or until the vegetables are tender. § Prepare the béchamel sauce. Let cool for 5–10 minutes. § Combine the béchamel with the Parmesan, eggs, vegetables, and mint. Season with salt and pepper. Mix well. § Grease a ring mold 10 in (25 cm) in diameter with the butter and sprinkle with bread crumbs. § Line the mold with the sliced zucchini by sticking them one by one to the butter and bread crumbs until the mold is covered. § Pour the mixture into the mold, taking care not to knock the zucchini off the sides of the mold. § Place the mold in a larger container filled with water and cook in a preheated oven at 400°F/200°C/gas 6 for 50 minutes. § Let stand for 10 minutes, then invert onto a serving dish.

■ INGREDIENTS

- 1¼ lb (600 g) zucchini (courgettes), thinly sliced
- 4 tablespoons extra-virgin olive oil
- 2 medium onions, 4 medium carrots, finely chopped together
- 1 quantity *Béchamel sauce* (see recipe p. 22)
- ½ cup (2 oz/60 g) Parmesan cheese, freshly grated
- 2 eggs, beaten until foamy
- 2 tablespoons fresh mint, finely chopped
- salt and freshly ground black pepper
- butter to grease the mold and bread crumbs

Wine: a dry white (Locorotondo)

Gratin soffice di cipolle
Fluffy onion gratin

Serves: 4-6; Preparation: 30 minutes; Cooking: 1½ hours; Level of difficulty: Simple

Boil the potatoes in their skins in a pot of salted water for about 25 minutes. Drain and cover to keep warm. § Place the onions, oil, half the butter, wine, water, stock cube, salt, and pepper in a saucepan, cover and simmer for 35 minutes, or until the onions are soft. § Peel the potatoes, chop coarsely, and mash. § Heat the milk in a saucepan and add the potatoes and the remaining butter (reserving 1 tablespoon) to make a smooth purée. Remove from heat and let cool for 10 minutes. § Combine the purée with the eggs, salt, and pepper. Stir in the Parmesan (reserving 2 tablespoons) and mix well. § Butter an ovenproof dish and spread with half the potato mixture in an even layer. § Drain the cooked onions of any liquid and spread over the potatoes. Sprinkle with the Gruyère and cover with the remaining potatoes. § Sprinkle with bread crumbs and Parmesan. § Bake in a preheated oven at 350°F/180°C/gas 4 for 25 minutes. § Serve hot as an entrée, light lunch, or side dish.

■ INGREDIENTS

- 3 lb (1.5 kg) potatoes
- 6 large onions, sliced
- 1 tablespoon extra-virgin olive oil
- ½ cup (4 oz/125 g) butter
- 1 cup (8 fl oz/250 ml) dry white wine
- ½ cup (4 fl oz/125 ml) water
- 1 vegetable stock cube
- salt and black pepper
- 1¼ cups (10 fl oz/300 ml) milk
- 3 eggs, beaten until foamy
- 1 cup (4 oz/125 g) Parmesan cheese, freshly grated
- 1 cup (4 oz/125 g) Gruyère cheese, freshly grated
- 2 tablespoons bread crumbs

Wine: a dry red (Refosco)

Right: *Gratin soffice di cipolla*

Ingredients

■ INGREDIENTS

- 1 medium Savoy cabbage
- 2 onions, 2 cloves garlic, finely chopped
- 2½ tablespoons extra-virgin olive oil
- 1¼ cups (8 oz/250 g) parboiled rice
- 1 lb (500 g) tomatoes, peeled and chopped
- 1 quantity *Béchamel sauce* (see recipe p. 22)
- 2 cups (8 oz/250 g) Gruyère cheese, grated
- 1 tablespoon butter

Wine: a dry red (Chianti)

Gratin delicato di verza e riso
Cabbage, rice and tomato gratin

Serves: 4; Preparation: 25 minutes; Cooking: 55 minutes; Level of difficulty: Simple

Cut the cabbage in half and then into strips. Blanch in salted, boiling water, drain well, and spread on a dishcloth to dry. § In a large skillet (frying pan), sauté the onion and garlic in the oil for 5 minutes. § Stir in the rice and season with salt and pepper. § Add the tomatoes and cook for 15 minutes, or until the rice is cooked. § Prepare the béchamel, adding half the Gruyère. § Grease an ovenproof dish and fill with alternate layers of cabbage and rice and tomatoes. § Cover with béchamel and sprinkle with the remaining cheese. Bake in a preheated oven at 350°F/180°C/gas 4 for 30 minutes.

Melanzane farcite piccanti

Stuffed eggplants with Provolone cheese

Serves: 4; Preparation: 30 minutes + 1 hour to degorge the eggplants; Cooking: 40 minutes; Level of difficulty: Simple

Cut the eggplants in half lengthwise and make crosswise slits in the pulp without piercing the skin. Sprinkle with the coarse salt and place the halves face upward in a large flat dish. Cover with another dish facing upward and put a weight on top. Leave for at least 1 hour. § Drain and rinse under running water, squeeze gently and place face down on paper towels to dry. § Mix the garlic, pancetta, and two Provolone cheeses in a bowl. § Place the eggplants in an ovenproof earthenware dish with half the oil. Press the eggplants open and push the filling in the slits made earlier with the knife. § Cover with the tomatoes and sprinkle with Parmesan. Season with pepper (don't add salt, as the eggplants have already absorbed enough). § Drizzle with the remaining oil. § Pour in the stock and cook over medium-low heat for 10–15 minutes. § Bake in a preheated oven at 350°F/180°C/gas 4 for 25–30 minutes. Baste with the stock frequently. § Serve hot as a main course.

■ INGREDIENTS

- 6 long eggplants (aubergines)
- 2 tablespoons coarse salt
- 8 cloves garlic, chopped
- ½ cup (2 oz/60 g) pancetta, diced
- 4 oz (125 g) each sharp and mild Provolone, diced
- 1½ lb (750 g) tomatoes, peeled and chopped
- freshly ground black pepper
- ⅓ cup (1½ oz/50 g) Parmesan cheese, freshly grated
- 4 tablespoons extra-virgin olive oil
- 1 cup (8 fl oz/250 ml) *Beef* or *Vegetable stock* (see recipes p. 20)

Wine: a dry white (Lugana di Verona)

Parmigiana di melanzane

Eggplant in tomato sauce with Parmesan and Mozzarella cheese

A classic Italian recipe, originally from Sicily. It is a hearty dish and can be served as a complete main course. Try replacing the eggplant with 3 pounds (1.5 kg) of zucchini (courgettes) for a lighter dish.

Serves: 6-8; Preparation: 15 minutes + 1 hour to degorge the eggplants; Cooking: 50 minutes; Level of difficulty: Simple

Peel the eggplants and cut in ¼-in (6-mm) thick slices and sprinkle with coarse salt. Place in a flat dish. Cover with another dish with a weight on top. Leave for at least 1 hour. § Drain and rinse in cold water. Pat dry with paper towels. § Prepare the tomato sauce. § Dredge the eggplants in the flour. § Heat the oil in a large sauté pan, dip the eggplant slices in the egg mixture and fry until golden brown. § Drain on paper towels. § Place a layer of tomato sauce in the bottom of an ovenproof dish and cover with a layer of eggplant and a layer of Mozzarella and Parmesan. Repeat until you have several layers of each. Reserve a little tomato sauce and Parmesan for the top. § Dot with butter and bake in a preheated oven at 350°F/180°C/gas 4 for 35 minutes. § Serve hot.

■ INGREDIENTS

- 3 large round eggplants (aubergines)
- 2 tablespoons coarse salt
- 2 quantities *Basic tomato sauce* (see recipe p. 16)
- all-purpose (plain) flour to dredge
- 4 eggs, beaten with a dash of salt
- 3 cups (24 fl oz/750 ml) oil, for frying
- 12 oz (350 g) Mozzarella cheese, thinly sliced
- 2½ cups (10 oz/300 g) Parmesan cheese, freshly grated
- 2 tablespoons butter

Wine: a dry red (Merlot di Aprilia)

Right: Parmigiana di melanzane

GRATIN DI BELGA E PROSCIUTTO
Belgian endives baked in béchamel sauce

■ INGREDIENTS

- 8 medium heads Belgian endives
- 3 tablespoons extra-virgin olive oil
- ½ cup (4 fl oz/125 ml) water
- salt
- 1 quantity *Béchamel sauce* (see recipe p. 22)
- salt and freshly ground black pepper
- 1 tablespoon butter to grease the pan
- 8 thick slices ham
- 1 cup (4 oz/125 g) Gruyère cheese, freshly grated

Wine: a dry red (Chianti Castelgreve)

Serves: 4; Preparation: 40 minutes; Cooking: 1 hour; Level of difficulty: Simple

Using a sharp knife, hollow out the base of the endives to remove the bitter part and ensure uniform cooking. § Place the heads in a large pan with the oil, water, and salt to taste. Cover and cook over medium heat for about 40 minutes. Drain well. § Prepare the béchamel sauce. § Wrap each endive in a slice of ham and arrange the heads in a greased ovenproof dish (place the part where the ham overlaps underneath). § Pour the béchamel over the rolls and sprinkle with the Gruyère. § Bake in a preheated oven at 350°F/180°C/gas 4 for 25 minutes, or until the topping is golden brown. § Serve hot as an entrée or main course.

POMODORI IN VERDE
Tomatoes baked with Parmesan, parsley, and garlic

■ INGREDIENTS

- 10 medium tomatoes
- 5 cloves garlic, finely chopped
- 1 cup (1 oz/30 g) parsley, finely chopped
- ½ cup (2 oz/60 g) bread crumbs
- ½ cup (2 oz/60 g) Parmesan cheese, freshly grated
- ½ cup (4 fl oz/125 ml) extra-virgin olive oil
- salt and freshly ground black pepper

Wine: a dry red (Bardolino)

Left: Pomodori in verde

Serves: 4-6; Preparation: 35 minutes; Cooking: 35 minutes; Level of difficulty: Simple

Cut the tomatoes in half, remove the seeds with your fingers, sprinkle with a little salt, and place upside down in a colander for 20 minutes. § Mix the garlic and parsley together in a bowl, add the bread crumbs and Parmesan, and, using a fork, work the oil in little by little. Season with salt and pepper. § Using a teaspoon, push the filling mixture into the tomato halves. Press it down with your fingers so that it sticks to the inside of the tomatoes (it will swell slightly in the oven and could overflow). § Place the filled tomatoes in a greased ovenproof dish and bake in a preheated oven at 350°F/180°C/gas 4 for 35 minutes. § Serve hot or warm as an appetizer, or as a side dish with roast beef. Perfect also with baked fish.

CRÊPES FARCITE CON BIETOLINA E CAPRINO
Crêpes stuffed with Swiss chard and goat's cheese

Serves: 6; Preparation: 60 minutes; Cooking: 30 minutes; Level of difficulty: Medium

Prepare the crêpes and set aside. § Cook the chard in a pot of salted water for 5 minutes. Drain, squeeze, and chop finely. § In a large skillet (frying pan), sauté the garlic in the butter until pale gold, then discard. § In the same skillet, sauté the chard with a dash of salt for 5 minutes. § Prepare the béchamel. § Spread the goat's cheese on the crêpes and grate a little nutmeg over the cheese. § Place 2 tablespoons of chard on half of each crêpe. § Fold the crêpes in half and then in half again to form triangles. § Grease an ovenproof dish and arrange the crêpes, overlapping, inside. § Pour the béchamel sauce over the top and sprinkle with the Gruyère. § Bake in a preheated oven at 350°F/180°C/gas 4 for 20–25 minutes. § Serve hot.

■ INGREDIENTS

- 1 quantity *Crêpes* (see recipe p. 22)
- 1½ lb (750 g) fresh Swiss chard (silver beet)
- salt and freshly ground black pepper
- 2 cloves garlic, cut in half
- 2 tablespoons butter
- 1 quantity *Béchamel sauce* (see recipe p. 22)
- 7 oz (200 g) fresh Caprino (goat's cheese)
- whole nutmeg, to grate
- ½ cup (2 oz/60 g) Gruyère cheese, freshly grated

Wine: a slightly sweet sparkling red (Brachetto d'Acqui)

FAGOTTINI DI MELANZANE ALLA CARNE
Eggplant stuffed with chicken, mortadella and ham

Serves: 4; Preparation: 1½ hours; Cooking: 45 minutes; Level of difficulty: Simple

Cut the eggplants in ¼-in (6-mm) thick slices, sprinkle with the coarse salt and place in a flat dish. Cover with another dish facing upward with a weight on top. Leave for at least 1 hour. § Drain and rinse under cold running water. Pat dry with paper towels. § Chop the chicken, mortadella, and ham in a food processor. Place in a bowl with the Parmesan, eggs, garlic, pepper, and parsley and mix well. § Heat the frying oil in a large skillet (frying pan) and fry the eggplant, turning the slices until they are golden brown. Drain on paper towels. § Arrange the slices on a clean work bench in pairs, crosswise one over the other. Place a little filling in the middle of each pair and fold the inner slice first, followed by the outer slice. Fasten with a wooden toothpick. § Sauté the onion in the olive oil in a braiser for 5 minutes. Add the tomatoes, season with salt and pepper and cook for 5 more minutes. § Add the stuffed eggplant to the sauce and bake in a preheated oven at 350°F/180°C/gas 4 for 30 minutes. Baste with the sauce from time to time. § Serve hot with toast rubbed with garlic, or boiled potatoes with a little of the tomato sauce.

■ INGREDIENTS

- 4 medium eggplants (aubergines)
- ¼ cup (2 oz/60 g) salt
- 10 oz (300 g) chicken breast
- 4 oz (125 g) mortadella
- 10 oz (300 g) ham
- 1 cup (4 oz/125 g) Parmesan cheese, freshly grated
- 1 egg + 1 yolk, beaten
- 2 tablespoons parsley, 3 cloves garlic, finely chopped
- freshly ground black pepper
- 2 cups (16 fl oz/500 ml) oil, for frying
- 1 medium onion, finely chopped
- 4 tablespoons extra-virgin olive oil
- 1 15-oz (450-g) can tomatoes

Wine: a dry red (Barolo)

Right: *Crêpes farcite con bietolina e caprino*

- 6 zucchini (courgettes)
- salt
- 1 egg + 1 yolk, beaten
- 4 tablespoons Parmesan cheese, freshly grated
- 12 amaretti cookies (macaroons)
- 2 tablespoons parsley
- 1 tablespoon butter
- 2 tablespoons bread crumbs
- 3 tablespoons extra-virgin olive oil

Wine: a dry white (Riesling)

Zucchine farcite agli amaretti
Zucchini stuffed with almond macaroons

Serves: 4; Preparation: 25 minutes; Cooking: 30 minutes; Level of difficulty: Simple

Cook the zucchini in a pot of salted, boiling water for 5 minutes. Drain and cool. § Cut in half lengthwise and, using a sharp knife, remove the pulp. § Crush the amaretti cookies and place in a bowl with the eggs, chopped zucchini pulp, Parmesan, finely chopped parsley, and salt. Blend well with a fork. § Fill the zucchini with the mixture and place in a buttered baking dish. § Sprinkle with the bread crumbs, drizzle with oil, and bake in a preheated oven at 350°F/180°C/gas 4 for 25 minutes. § Serve hot as an entrée.

Plum-cake di zucchine e fagiolini
Zucchini and green bean pie

A savory, Italian version of the celebrated British fruitcake.

Serves: 6; Preparation: 30 minutes; Cooking: 1¼ hours; Level of difficulty: Medium

Cook the zucchini and beans in a pot of salted, boiling water for 10 minutes. Drain, and cut the zucchini into wheels and the beans into pieces. Dry on a clean cotton dish towel. § Melt the butter and place in a bowl with two whole eggs, two yolks, and the sugar. Beat vigorously for 2 minutes with a whisk or fork. Stir in the flour, zucchini, beans, pine nuts, and baking powder. § Beat the remaining egg whites to stiff peaks and carefully fold into the mixture. § Grease a large loaf pan with butter and pour in the mixture. § Bake in a preheated oven at 350°F/180°C/gas 4 for 1 hour. § Remove from the pan when cool and cut into thick slices. § Serve as an appetizer, or a side dish with braised meats.

■ INGREDIENTS

• 10 oz (300 g) zucchini (courgettes)
• 8 oz (250 g) green beans, cleaned
• 1 teaspoon salt
• ⅔ cup (5 oz/150 g) butter
• 4 eggs
• ⅔ cup (4 oz/125 g) sugar
• 2½ cups (8 oz/250 g) all-purpose (plain) flour
• ⅔ cup (4 oz/125 g) pine nuts
• 2 teaspoons baking powder
• butter to grease the cake pan

Wine: a dry red (Sangiovese di Romagna)

Finocchi alla parmigiana
Baked fennel with Parmesan cheese

Serves: 4; Preparation: 15 minutes; Cooking: 25 minutes; Level of difficulty: Simple

Remove the outer leaves from each head of fennel, trim the tips and bottom, and cut in half. § Cook in salted, boiling water for 8–10 minutes, or until the fennel is cooked but still crunchy. § Drain, pat dry with paper towels, and cut into thick slices or wedges. § Melt three-quarters of the butter in a sauté pan over medium heat. Dredge the fennel slices lightly in the flour and fry in the butter until crisp and golden brown. § Place in a buttered baking dish. Sprinkle with salt, pepper, and Parmesan and dot with the remaining butter. § Bake in a preheated oven at 400°F/200°C/gas 6 for 15 minutes. § Serve hot as an entrée, or a side dish with oven-roasted fish or meat.

■ INGREDIENTS

• 5 large fennel bulbs
• salt and freshly ground black pepper
• ½ cup (4 oz/125 g) butter
• ⅓ cup (1¼ oz/40 g) all-purpose (plain) flour
• 1 cup (4 oz/125 g) Parmesan cheese, freshly grated

Wine: a dry white (Soave)

VARIATION
– For a richer dish: boil, slice and dry the fennel as above, then add 1 finely sliced small onion and brown with the fennel (add more butter if necessary). When brown, add 1½ cups (6 oz/180 g) diced ham, 4 tablespoons fresh cream, and season with salt and pepper. Cover and reduce over low heat for about 15 minutes. Sprinkle with 1½ cups (6 oz/180 g) freshly grated Parmesan and bake as above.

Right:
Porri gratinati al prosciutto

■ INGREDIENTS

- 2 lb (1 kg) fresh leeks
- salt and freshly ground
  black pepper
- 1 quantity *Béchamel sauce*
  (see recipe p. 22)
- 1 tablespoon butter
- 1 egg yolk
- 1 cup (4 oz/125 g) ham,
  finely chopped
- ½ cup (2 oz/60 g) Gruyère
  cheese, freshly grated

Wine: a dry white (Tocai di Lison)

PORRI GRATINATI AL PROSCIUTTO
Baked leeks with béchamel sauce and chopped ham

Serves: 4; Preparation: 15 minutes; Cooking: 45 minutes; Level of difficulty: Simple

Discard any withered leaves from the leeks and chop off the green tops. Cook in salted, boiling water for about 10 minutes, or until tender. § Prepare the béchamel and leave to cool. § Drain the leeks and sauté for 5 minutes in a skillet (frying pan) with the butter, salt, and pepper. Place in an ovenproof dish. § Combine the egg yolk and three-quarters of the ham with the béchamel, mix well, and pour over the leeks. Sprinkle with the Gruyère and remaining ham. § Bake in a preheated oven at 350°F/180°C/gas 4 for 20 minutes. § Serve hot as an entrée, or as a side dish with fish.

PATATE GRATINATE CON PROSCIUTTO E NOCI
Baked potatoes with béchamel, ham, and walnuts

Serves: 4-6; Preparation: 20 minutes; Cooking: 1 hour; Level of difficulty: Simple

Cook the potatoes in their skins in salted, boiling water for about 25 minutes. Drain and set aside to cool. § Prepare a rather thick béchamel sauce and stir in the Parmesan. § Peel the potatoes and cut in ½-in (1-cm) thick slices. Grease an ovenproof dish with half the butter and cover the bottom with a layer of potatoes. Fill in the gaps so that the bottom is sealed. § Cover with a layer of béchamel and sprinkle with the ham and chopped walnuts. Continue with another layer of potatoes and cover with the Mozzarella and a little béchamel sauce. Make a top layer of potatoes and cover with the remaining béchamel. Sprinkle with the bread crumbs and dot with the remaining butter. § Bake in a preheated oven at 350°F/180°C/gas 4 for 25 minutes. § Garnish with remaining walnut halves and serve hot as an entrée or main course.

TORTA DI ZUCCA E PATATE
Potato and pumpkin pie

Serves: 4; Preparation: 20 minutes; Cooking: 1¼ hours; Level of difficulty: Simple

Peel the pumpkin and cut it in slices. Cover with aluminum foil and bake in a preheated oven at 350°F/180°C/gas 4 for about 25 minutes, or until soft. § Boil the potatoes in their skins for about 25 minutes, drain, and peel. § Purée the potatoes and pumpkin together in a food processor. § Add half the butter, then the egg yolks and Parmesan. Mix rapidly, and season with salt and pepper. § Beat the egg whites to stiff peaks and fold them into the mixture. § Grease an ovenproof dish with butter and sprinkle with the bread crumbs. § Spread half the mixture evenly in the bottom of the dish and cover with the Mozzarella. Cover with the rest of the mixture. § Use a spoon to level, sprinkle with the Parmesan, and dot with the remaining butter. Bake in a preheated oven at 350°F/180°C/gas 4 for 50 minutes. § Serve hot with a green salad as a main course or light lunch, or as side dish with roast lamb or barbecued pork.

■ INGREDIENTS

• 2 lb (1 kg) boiling potatoes
• salt and freshly ground black pepper
• 1 quantity *Béchamel sauce* (see recipe p. 22)
• ½ cup (2 oz/60 g) Parmesan cheese, freshly grated
• 2 tablespoons butter
• 1¾ cups (7 oz/200 g) ham, finely chopped
• 1½ cups (6 oz/180 g) shelled walnuts, almost all coarsely chopped
• 7 oz (200 g) Mozzarella cheese, thinly sliced
• 1 tablespoon bread crumbs

Wine: a dry red (Dolcetto d'Alba)

■ INGREDIENTS

• 1 lb (500 g) pumpkin,
• 1 lb (500 g) boiling potatoes
• ⅓ cup (3½ oz/100 g) butter
• 4 eggs, separated
• 1 cup (4 oz/125 g) Parmesan cheese, freshly grated
• salt and freshly ground black pepper
• 2 tablespoons bread crumbs
• 12 oz (350 g) Mozzarella cheese, sliced

Wine: a dry red (Barbaresco)

Right: *Patate gratinate con prosciutto e noci*

Cipolle farcite di riso integrale
Onions stuffed with brown rice and oregano

Serves: 4; Preparation: 25 minutes; Cooking: 1½ hours; Level of difficulty: Medium

Cook the rice in a large pot of salted, boiling water and drain. § Peel the onions, trim the bottoms and slice off the tops. Cook for 7–8 minutes in a pot of salted, boiling water. Set aside to cool. § Hollow out the onions with a sharp knife leaving a ½-in (1-cm) thick shell. Set the pulp aside. § Beat the eggs in a bowl, and add the rice, half the oregano, Parmesan, Pecorino, chopped olives, salt, and pepper. Mix well. § Spoon the filling into the onions and sprinkle with the remaining oregano. § In a bowl, mix 4 tablespoons of onion pulp, the halved olives, 1 tablespoon of olive oil, salt, and pepper, and pour into an ovenproof dish. § Arrange the stuffed onions in the dish and pour the remaining oil, the wine, and stock over the top. Dot each onion with butter. § Bake in a preheated oven at 350°F/180°C/gas 4 for 40 minutes. § Serve hot as an entrée.

■ INGREDIENTS

- 1¼ cups (8 oz/250 g) brown rice
- 8 large onions
- salt and pepper
- 3 eggs
- 2 tablespoons oregano
- ½ cup (2 oz/60 g) Parmesan cheese, freshly grated
- 1 cup (4 oz/125 g) Pecorino romano cheese, freshly grated
- 1½ cups (6 oz/180 g) pitted black olives
- 4 tablespoons extra-virgin olive oil
- 1 cup (8 oz/250 ml) dry white wine
- 1 cup (8 oz/250 ml) *Vegetable stock* (see recipe p. 20)
- 2 tablespoons butter

Wine: a dry red (Freisa d'Asti)

Ciuffetti di patate e spinaci
Spinach and potato appetizers

Serves: 8; Preparation: 30 minutes; Cooking: 1 hour; Level of difficulty: Medium

Boil the potatoes in their skins for about 25 minutes. § Drain, peel, and mash. § Put the purée in a saucepan and add two-thirds of the butter, the salt, pepper, nutmeg, and milk. Place over low heat and, stirring constantly, dry out excess moisture. Set aside to cool. § Cook the spinach in a pot of salted, boiling water until tender (3–4 minutes if frozen, 8–10 minutes if fresh). Drain well and squeeze out excess moisture. Chop finely. § Beat the egg and one yolk together and mix well with the potato purée. § Divide the potato purée in two and mix the spinach and a dash of salt into one half. If the mixture is too moist, stir over low heat to dry. § Grease a baking sheet, spoon the potato mixture into a pastry bag, and squeeze out into walnut-sized rosettes. Repeat with the spinach mixture. § Beat the remaining egg yolk and brush the rosettes with it. § Bake in a preheated oven at 400°F/200°C/gas 6 for 20 minutes. § Scoop the rosettes off the sheet with a spatula and serve hot as appetizers.

■ INGREDIENTS

- 2 lb (1 kg) boiling potatoes
- ½ cup (4 oz/125 g) butter
- salt and freshly ground black pepper
- dash of nutmeg
- 1 cup (8 fl oz/250 ml) milk
- 1 lb (500 g) fresh or frozen spinach
- 1 egg + 2 yolks

Wine: a dry sparkling red (Lambrusco di Sorbara)

Right:
Cipolle farcite di riso integrale

■ INGREDIENTS

- 1 quantity *Puff pastry* (see recipe p. 18)
- 6 large onions, thinly sliced
- 4 tablespoons butter
- 2 cups (16 fl oz/500 ml) dry white wine
- 1 cup (8 fl oz/250 ml) *Vegetable stock* (see recipe p. 20) or water
- 1 beef stock cube
- 2½ cups (9½ oz/280 g) dried beans, such as garbanzo beans (chickpeas)
- ¾ cup (7 oz/200 g) fresh creamy cheese, such as Robiola or Mascarpone
- 1 teaspoon fresh mint

Wine: a dry white (Tocai)

■ INGREDIENTS

- 1 quantity *Puff pastry* (see recipe p. 18)
- 2 red bell peppers
- 4 zucchini (courgettes)
- 4 large carrots
- salt and freshly ground black pepper
- 3 tablespoons extra-virgin olive oil
- 2 tablespoons butter
- ½ cup (4 oz/125 g) white wine
- 2½ cups (9½ oz/280 g) dried beans, such as garbanzo beans (chickpeas)

Wine: a dry white (Est! Est!! Est!!! di Montefiascone)

Left: *Crostata di verdure miste*

CROSTATA DI CIPOLLA
Onion pie

Serves: 6; Preparation: 20 minutes + 1½ hours for the pastry; Cooking: 1 hour; Level of difficulty: Simple

Prepare the pastry dough. § In a large skillet (frying pan), sauté the onions in the butter. Season with salt and pepper. When the onions are soft, add the wine, followed by the vegetable stock and beef stock cube. § Simmer over low heat for 30 minutes, or until the onions are creamy. If the liquid evaporates during cooking, add water or more stock. § On a clean, lightly floured work bench, roll out the pastry dough and use it to line a greased ovenproof 10-in (25-cm) pie plate. Prick the dough with a fork. § Cover the pie crust with a sheet of aluminum foil, weigh it down with the dried beans, and bake in a preheated oven at 375°F/190°C/gas 5 for 35 minutes. § Remove the foil and beans and bake for 10 minutes more. § Set aside to cool, then spread with creamy cheese. § Spread a layer of onion over the cheese and sprinkle with the mint. § Serve hot or at room temperature.

CROSTATA DI VERDURE MISTE
Vegetable pie

Serves: 6; Preparation: 20 minutes + 1½ hours for the pastry; Cooking: 1 hour; Level of difficulty: Simple

Prepare the pastry dough. § Cut the bell peppers in thin strips, the zucchini in wheels, and the carrots in ribbons. § Sauté the bell peppers, a dash of salt, and the oil in a skillet (frying pan) over high heat for 10 minutes, stirring frequently. Take the bell peppers out and set aside. § Use the same oil to sauté the zucchini with a dash of salt. Remove from the skillet and set aside. § Use a paper towel to eliminate the oil in the skillet. Put the butter, carrots, wine, and a pinch of salt in it and cook until the liquid has evaporated and the carrots are tender. Set the carrots aside. § On a clean, lightly floured work bench, roll out the pastry dough and use it to line a greased ovenproof pie plate 10 in (25 cm) in diameter. Prick the dough with a fork. § Cover the pie crust with a sheet of aluminum foil, weigh it down with the dried beans, and bake in a preheated oven at 375°F/190°C/gas 5 for 35 minutes. § Remove the foil and beans and bake for 10 minutes more. § Garnish with the vegetables and serve as an appetizer, or with a platter of fresh cheeses (Ricotta, Mozzarella, Stracchino, Robiola, Caprino, or Mascarpone) as a light lunch.

CROSTATA DI BROCCOLI E PORRI
Broccoli and leek pie

Both the broccoli and leek pie and the pea and artichoke pie
(see variation) freeze well. Prepare them ahead of time.
They make a delicious lunch for unexpected guests.

Serves: 6; Preparation: 1 hour + 1 hour for the pastry; Cooking: 1½ hours; Level of difficulty: Medium

Prepare the pastry dough and set it aside in the refrigerator. § Cut the root and the green tops off the leeks and chop the white parts into fairly thin wheels. § Put the leeks in a sauté pan with the oil, cover and cook for 15 minutes. Remove from heat and set aside. § Dry the oil in the pan with paper towels and sauté the pancetta until crispy and brown. Set aside. § Divide the broccoli into florets with ½-in (1-cm) stems and cook in a pot of salted, boiling water for 7–10 minutes, or until cooked. § Roll out the pastry dough and use it to line a greased 10-in (25-cm) pie plate. Press the dough into the bottom and sides so it sticks to the plate. Prick well with a fork. Cover the pie crust with a sheet of aluminum foil and weigh it down with the dried beans. § Bake in a preheated oven at 350°F/180°C/gas 4 for 15 minutes, remove the foil and garbanzo beans and bake for 5 minutes more. § In the meantime, beat the eggs in a bowl and add the milk, cream, Parmesan, salt, and pepper. Beat with a whisk until frothy. § Put the leeks and broccoli in the baked pie shell, sprinkle with the pancetta, and pour the eggs and cheese over the top. § Bake in a preheated oven at 350°F/180°C/gas 4, turning the plate from time to time to make sure the pie cooks evenly. After 35 minutes check if the cream is cooked by sticking a toothpick into it; if it comes out damp, cook for 5–10 minutes more. § Serve hot as an entrée or snack.

■ INGREDIENTS

- 1 quantity *Plain pastry* (see recipe p. 18)
- 2 medium leeks
- 1½ tablespoons extra-virgin olive oil
- 1¼ cups (5 oz/150 g) diced pancetta
- 1 lb (500 g) broccoli
- 1 tablespoon butter
- salt and freshly ground black pepper
- 2½ cups (9½ oz/280 g) dried beans, such as garbanzo beans (chickpeas)
- 3 eggs + 2 yolks
- 1½ cups (12 fl oz/375 ml) milk
- 1 cup (8 fl oz/250 ml) heavy (double) cream
- ¾ cup (3 oz/90 g) Parmesan cheese, freshly grated

Wine: a dry white
(Isonzo Sauvignon)

VARIATION
— An alternative pie can be made by replacing the leeks and broccoli with peas and artichokes. Prepare the peas (8 oz/250 g) and 4 artichokes as indicated in the recipes *Piselli primavera al prezzemolo e prosciutto* (see p. 48) and *Spezzatino di carciofi* (see p. 38). The vegetables should be well drained of cooking juices before placing them in the pie shell. Cover with the eggs and cheese and bake and serve as above.

Right:
Crostata di broccoli e porri

Fried Vegetables

Even in tolerant Italy, serving crispy-fried golden vegetables is considered rather sinful. But by following one or two simple rules (see page 27 for instructions on how to fry food), the damage can be kept to a minimum. Fried vegetables need to be eaten hot, so prepare them ahead of time and serve them as you cook.

ZUCCA FRITTA ALLA MENTA E PINOLI
Fried pumpkin marinated with mint and pine nuts

Serves: 4; Preparation: 20 minutes + 3 hours marinating; Cooking: 30 minutes; Level of difficulty: Simple

Cut the pumpkin into bite-sized pieces and flour lightly. § Heat the frying oil to very hot and fry the pumpkin a few pieces at a time for 7–8 minutes. When the pieces are cooked, drain on paper towels. § Clean the oil, top up if necessary, and repeat until all the pumpkin is cooked. § Place on a serving dish and sprinkle with the garlic, half the mint, anchovy fillets, salt, and pepper. Dress with the olive oil and vinegar, and mix carefully. Set aside to marinate for at least 3 hours. § Add the pine nuts and remaining mint just before serving.

■ INGREDIENTS

- 2 lb (1 kg) pumpkin, peeled
- ¾ cup (3 oz/90 g) all-purpose (plain) flour
- 2 cups (16 fl oz/500 ml) oil, for frying
- 3 cloves garlic, sliced
- 30 fresh mint leaves
- 16 anchovy fillets, crumbled
- salt and freshly ground black pepper
- 3 tablespoons extra-virgin olive oil
- 2 tablespoons apple vinegar
- ⅓ cup (2 oz/60 g) pine nuts, sautéed in a little oil for 2–3 minutes

Wine: a light, dry white (Malvasia)

POMODORI VERDI FRITTI
Crispy-fried green tomatoes

This dish is comes from Tuscany, where it is served often throughout the summer months.

Serves: 4-6; Preparation: 15 minutes; Cooking: 40-50 minutes; Level of difficulty: Simple

Cut the tomatoes into ½-in (1-cm) thick slices. Discard the first and last slices which have skin on one side. § Place four bowls side by side and fill the first with the flour, the second with the beaten eggs and beer, and the last two with the bread crumbs. § Heat the frying oil in a large skillet (frying pan) until very hot. § Dip the tomato slices into the flour; make sure they are well-covered and shake off any excess. Flour all the slices and set them on paper towels. Don't lay the floured slices on top of each other. § Dip the slices in the egg, turn a couple of times, drain and pass to the first bowl of bread crumbs. Turn several times until they are well-coated. § Repeat with the second bowl of bread crumbs (which are drier). § Place a few slices in the hot oil and fry for about 10 minutes, or until they are golden brown. Turn them over carefully at least twice using tongs or two forks. § Clean the oil of any residue and top up if necessary. Continue to fry until all the tomatoes are cooked. § Drain the fried slices on paper towels and sprinkle with salt. § Serve hot on a heated serving dish as an appetizer, or side dish with mixed grilled meats.

■ INGREDIENTS

- 6 large green tomatoes
- 1 cup (4 oz/125 g) all-purpose (plain) flour
- 4 eggs, beaten
- 5 cups (1¼ lb/625 g) fine bread crumbs
- ⅓ cup (3½ fl oz/100 ml) beer
- 2 cups (16 fl oz/500 ml) oil, for frying
- salt

Wine: a dry red (Chianti Classico)

Right:
Pomodori verdi fritti

■ INGREDIENTS

- 1 quantity *Plain pastry* (see recipe p. 18)
- 12 oz (350 g) fresh or frozen Swiss chard (silver beet)
- 12 oz (350 g) fresh or frozen spinach
- salt and freshly ground black pepper
- 2 eggs + 1 yolk
- 1 cup (8 oz/250 g) Ricotta cheese, crumbled
- ⅔ cup (5 oz/150 g) Mozzarella cheese, diced
- 1 cup (4 oz/125 g) Parmesan cheese, freshly grated
- 2 cups oil, for frying

Wine: a young, dry red (Rosso di Montalcino)

FAGOTTINI DI BIETOLA E SPINACI
Swiss chard and spinach fritters

Serves: 6; Preparation: 30 minutes + 1 hour for the pastry; Cooking: 50 minutes; Level of difficulty: Simple

Prepare the pastry dough. § Cook the chard and spinach in a pot of salted, boiling water until tender (3–4 minutes if frozen, 8–10 minutes if fresh). Drain, cool under cold running water, squeeze out excess moisture, and chop finely. § Beat the 2 eggs in a bowl and add the Ricotta, Mozzarella, Parmesan, salt, and pepper, and mix well. § Add the chard and spinach and mix well. § Roll the pastry dough out on a clean, floured work surface until very thin. Cut into 4-in (10-cm) squares. § Place a little filling at the center of each and fold in half. Beat the remaining egg yolk and brush the edges of each square before pressing firmly to seal. § Heat the frying oil in a large skillet (frying pan) until very hot. § Fry the fritters in the oil for about 10 minutes, or until golden brown. Turn using tongs or two spoons. § Serve hot as an appetizer.

■ INGREDIENTS

- 1 small cauliflower (about 1 lb/500 g), divided in florets
- salt and freshly ground black pepper
- 3 eggs, beaten until foamy
- ¼ cup (2 fl oz/60 ml) beer
- 2 cups (16 fl oz/500 ml) oil, for frying
- 1 cup (4 oz/125 g) all-purpose (plain) flour
- 1 cup (8 fl oz/250 ml) white wine vinegar
- 2 scallions (spring onions), finely chopped
- 1 teaspoon fresh or ½ teaspoon dry thyme

Wine: a dry red (Pinot Nero)

CAVOLFIORE FRITTO MARINATO
Fried cauliflower florets served with vinegar marinade

Serves: 4; Preparation: 15 minutes; Cooking: 40 minutes; Level of difficulty: Simple

Cook the cauliflower florets in a pot of salted, boiling water for 4–5 minutes, or until just tender. Drain well, and place on a cotton dishcloth to dry. § Combine the beaten eggs with the beer. § Heat the frying oil in a large skillet (frying pan) until very hot. § Place the flour in a bowl, dip the florets in, turn a few times and shake off excess. § When the oil is hot, dip about 10 florets in the egg mixture. Coat well and transfer to the pan. § Turn a couple of times with two forks or tongs. Fry for about 10 minutes, or until golden brown all over. § Remove from the skillet and drain on paper towels. § Repeat until all the florets are fried. Sprinkle with salt. § To prepare the marinade, place the vinegar in a small saucepan with the scallions. Boil for 5–6 minutes, then add the thyme, and remove from heat. Pour into a serving bowl. § Serve the marinade and cauliflower florets hot as an appetizer, or as a side dish with fried chicken or oven-roasted fish.

Left: Cavolfiore fritto marinato

CROCCHETTE DI POMODORO
Tomato croquettes

■ INGREDIENTS

• 10 oz (300 g) tomatoes
• ⅔ cup (5 oz/150 g) Ricotta cheese, crumbled
• 1 egg (beaten until foamy) + 1 yolk
• 1½ tablespoons parsley, finely chopped
• dash of nutmeg
• salt and freshly ground black pepper
• 1 cup (4 oz/125 g) all-purpose (plain) flour
• 1 cup (4 oz/125 g) bread crumbs
• 3 cups (24 fl oz/750 ml) oil, for frying

Wine: a dry, fruity white (Vermentino)

Serves: 4; Preparation: 20 minutes; Cooking: 40 minutes; Level of difficulty: Medium

Peel the tomatoes, squeeze out the seeds, chop coarsely, and set in a colander to drain. § Place the Ricotta and egg yolk in a bowl and mix to a smooth paste. § Add the tomatoes, parsley, nutmeg, salt, and pepper and mix well. § Prepare 3 separate bowls: one with the flour, one with the egg, and one with the bread crumbs. § Heat the frying oil in a large skillet (frying pan) until very hot. § Shape the mixture into croquettes about 2 in (5 cm) long and 1 in (2.5 cm) thick. If the mixture is not firm enough, add 1–2 tablespoons of dry bread crumbs or freshly grated Parmesan cheese. § Roll the croquettes in the flour, dip in the egg, and roll in the bread crumbs. Fry a few at a time for about 10 minutes, or until golden brown. Turn with tongs or a fork during cooking. § Use a slotted spoon to scoop them out and drain on paper towels. § Serve hot as appetizers, or a side dish with fried meat or fish.

FUNGHI PORCINI FRITTI
Fried porcini mushrooms

■ INGREDIENTS

• 1¼ lb (600 g) fresh porcini mushrooms
• 1 cup (4 fl oz/125 g) all-purpose (plain) flour
• 3 cups (24 fl oz/750 ml) oil, for frying
• salt

Wine: a dry red (Collio di Pinot Nero)

This recipe calls for fresh, high-quality porcini mushrooms. If you can't get them, use fresh brown cremini or white mushrooms in their place.

Serves: 4; Preparation: 15 minutes; Cooking: 25 minutes; Level of difficulty: Simple

Trim the roots from the mushrooms and carefully peel the bottom of the stem if discolored or dirty. § Detach the stems from the caps and rinse under cold running water, removing any dirt with your fingers. Set aside to dry on paper towels. § Cut the stems and caps in slices about ¼-in (6-mm) thick. § Dredge the slices in the flour, coating well, and shake to eliminate any excess. § Heat the frying oil in a large skillet (frying pan) until very hot. Fry the mushrooms a few pieces at a time until golden brown. Cook all the stems first, then the caps. § Drain on paper towels, sprinkle with salt, and serve as an appetizer or side dish.

Right: *Funghi porcini fritti*

Salvia fritta
Fried fresh sage leaves

Don't use an iron skillet to fry the leaves because it could react chemically with the sage.

Serves: 4; Preparation: 10 minutes; Cooking: 5 minutes; Level of difficulty: Simple

Wash the leaves, pat dry with paper towels, and dredge in the flour. § Dip in the egg and coat well with bread crumbs. § Heat the frying oil in a large skillet (frying pan) to very hot and add half the leaves. They will turn golden brown almost instantly. Turn once, then scoop out with a slotted spoon. Drain on paper towels. § Sprinkle with salt and serve as an appetizer or snack. For a sweeter version, add 1 teaspoon of sugar to the salt before sprinkling.

■ INGREDIENTS

- 40 large fresh sage leaves
- 2 tablespoons all-purpose (plain) flour
- 1 large egg, beaten until foamy with a pinch of salt
- 1½ cups (6 oz/180 g) bread crumbs
- 2 cups (16 fl oz/500 ml) oil, for frying

Wine: a dry (or sweet) sparkling white (Asti Spumante)

■ INGREDIENTS

- 3 lb (1.5 kg) boiling
  potatoes
- salt and freshly ground
  black pepper
- 1 lb (500 g) fresh or
  12 oz (350 g) frozen
  spinach
- 1 egg + 1 yolk, beaten
- ½ cup (2 oz/60 g)
  Parmesan cheese, freshly
  grated
- 5 oz (150 g) Taleggio or
  Fontina cheese, cut in ¼-
  in (6-mm) cubes
- 2 cups (8 oz/250 g)
  bread crumbs
- 3 cups (24 fl oz/750 ml)
  oil, for frying

*Wine: a dry white
(Pinot Grigio)*

Crocchette di spinaci
Spinach croquettes

Serves: 4-6; Preparation: 30 minutes; Cooking: 1 hour; Level of difficulty: Simple

Cook the potatoes in their skins in a pot of salted, boiling water for about 25 minutes. Drain, peel, and mash. § Cook the spinach in a pot of salted, boiling water until tender (3–4 minutes if frozen, 8–10 minutes if fresh). Drain, cool under cold running water, squeeze out excess moisture, and chop finely. § Combine with the potatoes and mix well. § Put the eggs in a bowl with the salt, pepper, potatoes, spinach, and Parmesan and blend with a fork until smooth. § Place a tablespoonful of the mixture in the palm of your hand. Press a cube of cheese into the center and close the mixture round to make an oblong croquette. The cheese must be completely covered. Roll in the bread crumbs. § Heat the frying oil in a large skillet (frying pan) until very hot. § Fry the croquettes a few at a time, turning them in the oil so that they are golden brown all over. Remove with a slotted spoon and drain on paper towels. Repeat until all the croquettes are cooked. § Serve hot as appetizers, or with a mixed salad as a main course.

> VARIATION
> – Replace the spinach with porcini mushrooms (see recipe *Funghi porcini trifolati* p. 46). In this case, either omit the cheese or use Mozzarella.

■ INGREDIENTS

- 1¼ lb (600 g) potatoes
- 2 eggs, beaten
- 2 tablespoons all-purpose
  (plain) flour
- salt and freshly ground
  black pepper
- 2 cups (16 fl oz/500 ml)
  oil, for frying

*Wine: a dry rosé
(Lagrein Rosato)*

Frittelle di patate
Potato patties

Serves: 4; Preparation: 15 minutes; Cooking: 15-20 minutes; Level of difficulty: Simple

Peel the potatoes and grate into julienne strips with a grater. Rinse them in plenty of cold water, drain well, and spread on a cotton dishcloth to dry. § Place the eggs, flour, salt, and pepper in a bowl, add the potatoes and mix well. If the mixture is not firm enough, add a little more flour to thicken. § Heat the frying oil in a large skillet (frying pan) until very hot. Place 6–8 widely separated tablespoons of the mixture in the oil. Brown on one side then turn carefully and brown on the other. § Scoop the patties out with a slotted spoon and drain on paper towels. § Serve hot as appetizers, or as a side dish with fried meat or fish dishes.

Left: *Crocchette di spinaci*

Fritto misto estivo
Mixed fried summer vegetables

In winter, replace the summer vegetables with artichoke wedges, carrots and potatoes cut in sticks, sliced fennel, and florets of broccoli. The procedure is the same except that the fennel and broccoli must be cooked first in salted, boiling water until just tender and dried on paper towels before flouring.

Serves: 4-6; Preparation: 20 minutes; Cooking: 50 minutes; Level of difficulty: Simple

Cut the zucchini in half crosswise, and cut each half in quarters lengthwise. If you are using long eggplants, slice in ¼ in (6 mm) wheels. If you are using the larger, pear-shaped eggplants, cut in ¼-in (6-mm) thick slices and cut each slice in halves or quarters (depending on how big they are). § Trim the stems of the zucchini flowers and wash carefully. Place on paper towels to dry. § Put the flour in a large bowl next to another containing the eggs and beer. § Heat the frying oil in a large skillet (frying pan) until very hot. § Flour the vegetables, shake off any excess, and dip in the egg. Shake off excess egg. § Begin frying a few pieces at a time; if there are too many in the skillet at once they will stick together. § Turn the vegetables as they turn brown. When all the pieces are golden brown, scoop them up with a slotted spoon and drain on paper towels. Repeat until all the vegetables are cooked. § Sprinkle with salt and serve hot as an entrée, or as a side dish with fried or roast meat or fish dishes.

■ INGREDIENTS

- 4 zucchini (courgettes)
- 4 eggplants (aubergines)
- 12 large zucchini (courgette) flowers
- 2 cups (7 oz/200 g) all-purpose (plain) flour
- 4 eggs, beaten
- ⅓ cup (3½ fl oz/100 ml) beer
- 3 cups (24 fl oz/750 ml) oil, for frying
- salt

Wine: a dry white (Frascati)

Anelli di cipolla croccanti
Crispy-fried onion rings

Serves: 4; Preparation: 20 minutes + 1 hour for the batter; Cooking: 20 minutes; Level of difficulty: Simple

Prepare the batter. § Peel the onions and chop in ¼ in (6 mm) slices. Separate the rings and leave them to dry for a few minutes. § Heat the frying oil in a large skillet (frying pan) until very hot. § Beat the egg white to stiff peaks and fold into the batter. § Dip the rings in the batter one by one, let the excess batter drip off, and fry to golden brown, turning once or twice with tongs or a fork. Remember to keep the oil clean. § Drain on paper towels. § Serve hot as an appetizer.

■ INGREDIENTS

- 4 medium onions
- 1 quantity *Batter* (see recipe p. 20)
- 1 egg white
- 2 cups (16 fl oz/500 ml) oil, for frying

Wine: a dry, sparkling white (Prosecco di Conegliano)

Right:
Fritto misto estivo

GRILLED VEGETABLES

Cooking vegetables quickly under a broiler (grill), in a grill pan, or over a barbecue enhances their natural flavors. Experiment with the dishes here, then try grilling a selection of different vegetables together and serve with oil, finely chopped parsley, and garlic as a light and healthy lunch, or as a second course after a hearty pasta dish.

Involtini di zucchine grigliate
Stuffed zucchini rolls

Serves: 4; Preparation: 15 minutes; Cooking: 10 minutes; Level of difficulty: Simple

Cut the tops off the zucchini and cut lengthwise in ⅛-in (3-mm) slices. § Heat the grill pan until hot and cook the slices over medium-high heat for about 3 minutes on each side. Transfer to a plate. § Put the Caprino in a bowl and mash with a fork. Add the tuna and mix well. Season with salt and pepper, add the parsley, and blend vigorously until the mixture is smooth. § Place 2–3 teaspoons of filling on each zucchini slice, add some basil and roll up, fastening with a wooden toothpick. § Place the rolls on a serving dish. Sprinkle with capers and basil leaves, and drizzle with oil. § Serve at room temperature as appetizers.

■ INGREDIENTS

- 4 large, long zucchini (courgettes)
- 1½ cups (12 oz/350 g) Caprino (goat's) cheese
- 1 cup (7 oz/200 g) tuna, packed in olive oil, crumbled
- salt and freshly ground black pepper
- 1 tablespoon parsley, finely chopped
- 1½ tablespoons capers
- 15 basil leaves, torn
- 3 tablespoons extra-virgin olive oil

Wine: a dry white (Verduzzo)

Melanzane alla griglia in olio piccante
Grilled eggplants in oil and chili sauce

Eggplants are now available throughout the year, but for successful grilling be sure to use them in their natural season—summer—when their full, flagrant flavor is at its peak. They can be served al naturale (sprinkled with a little finely chopped parsley and garlic and bathed in olive oil) or with the delicious spicy sauce given here. For an even richer flavor, sprinkle the grilled eggplants with 1 tablespoon of fresh oregano. Covered with oil, they will keep in the refrigerator for several days.

Serves: 4-6; Preparation: 15 minutes; Cooking: 20 minutes; Level of difficulty: Simple

Chop the ends off the eggplants and cut in ½-in (1-cm) thick slices. § Heat the grill pan to very hot and place the slices on it. Press them down with a fork so the eggplant adheres to the pan. Turn the slices after about 30 seconds (they will have black stripes on the cooked side). Eggplant cooks quickly so don't let the slices dry out. § As soon as the pulp is soft, remove from the grill pan and arrange on the serving dish. § Put the chilies, salt, and pepper in the oil and beat with a fork for a few minutes. Cover and set aside. § When the eggplants are all cooked, pour the spicy oil over the top and garnish with the basil leaves. § Serve warm or at room temperature as an appetizer, or side dish with mixed barbecued meats or fish.

■ INGREDIENTS

- 4 large round eggplants (aubergines)
- 2 hot chili peppers, finely chopped, or 1 teaspoon crushed chilies
- salt and freshly ground black pepper
- 1 cup (8 fl oz/250 ml) extra-virgin olive oil
- 10 fresh basil leaves, torn

Wine: a dry red (Rossesse di Dolceacqua)

Right: Melanzane alla griglia in olio piccante

INGREDIENTS

- 8 medium ripe tomatoes
- salt and freshly ground black pepper
- 2 heaped tablespoons oregano
- 16 fresh basil leaves, torn
- 4 tablespoons extra-virgin olive oil to drizzle

*Wine: a dry red
(Refosco)*

Pomodori rossi alla griglia
Grilled tomatoes

Serves: 4; Preparation: 10 minutes; Cooking: 15 minutes; Level of difficulty: Simple

Cut the tomatoes in half and squeeze out the seeds with your fingers. Place the halves upside down for 2–3 minutes. § Heat the grill pan to hot. § Sprinkle the tomatoes with salt, pepper, and oregano. § Place the tomatoes on the grill pan skin-side-down and cook over high heat without turning for about 15 minutes, or until they are cooked. § Remove from the pan, place a basil leaf in the center of each, and drizzle with the oil. § Serve hot on toasted whole-wheat or homemade bread as an appetizer, or as a side dish with grilled meat or fish.

■ INGREDIENTS

- 2 long zucchini
  (courgettes)
- 1 long eggplant
  (aubergine)
- 1 medium onion
- 1 small red, 1 small yellow,
  and 1 small green bell
  pepper (capsicum)
- 2½ tablespoons extra-
  virgin olive oil
- salt and freshly ground
  black pepper
- ½ teaspoon paprika
- juice of ½ lemon
- 1 teaspoon dried or
  1 tablespoon chopped
  fresh herbs (oregano,
  mint, or thyme)

Wine: a dry, sparkling white
(Prosecco di Conegliano)

Spiedini misti variopinti
Skewered mixed vegetables

Serves: 4; Preparation: 25 minutes + 2 hours marinating; Cooking: 20 minutes; Level of difficulty: Simple

Cut the zucchini in wheels. Chop the eggplant in thick slices, then divide them in 4. Divide the onion in 4 wedges, then cut each wedge in half. Cut the bell peppers in 1-in (2.5-cm) squares. § Thread the vegetable pieces onto wooden skewers. Set them on a plate. Prepare at least two skewers per person. § Place the oil, salt, pepper, paprika, lemon juice, and herbs in a small bowl and beat vigorously with a fork until the sauce is well mixed. § Pour over the skewers, cover with aluminum foil, and marinate in the refrigerator for 2 hours. § Heat a grill pan over high heat until very hot, drain the skewers, and place half of them in the pan. Cook for about 10 minutes, turning them so that they brown on all sides. Repeat with the remaining skewers. § Serve hot as a side dish with grilled meats or fish, or garnish with squares of grilled polenta and serve as an appetizer.

■ INGREDIENTS

- 4 heads fresh Belgian
  endives
- 4 heads red radicchio
- salt and freshly ground
  black pepper
- 4 tablespoons extra-virgin
  olive oil

Wine: a dry white
(Soave Classico)

Insalata belga e radicchio rosso alla griglia
Grilled Belgian endives and radicchio

Belgian endives and radicchio are both part of the chicory family. Radicchio can be very bitter; try to buy the long tapering variety with mottled red leaves called Radicchio di Treviso.

Serves: 4; Preparation: 10 minutes; Cooking: 15 minutes; Level of difficulty: Simple

Trim the bases of the Belgian endives and radicchio, remove any withered leaves, and cut the heads in half. § Heat a grill pan until very hot, then lower heat to medium, and place the Belgian endives and radicchio in it. § Cover with a lid or sheet of aluminum foil during the first 5 minutes of cooking, then uncover and turn often until cooked. § Arrange the endives and radicchio in alternate red and white strips in a preheated serving dish. Sprinkle with salt and pepper and drizzle with the oil. § For a delicious and healthy light lunch, serve hot on a bed of boiled brown rice and garnish with wedges of cherry tomatoes and freshly grated Pecorino romano cheese.

Left:
Spiedini misti variopinti

PORCINI ALLA GRIGLIA
Grilled wild mushrooms on toast with herb butter

The Italian recipe calls for fresh porcini, but you can use other wild mushrooms in their place. Experiment with shiitake, chanterelle, hedgehog, cremini, or portobello mushrooms (or a mixture).

Serves: 4; Preparation: 10 minutes; Cooking: 10-15 minutes; Level of difficulty: Simple

Remove any dirt from the mushrooms, trim the tough parts off the stems, and rinse carefully under cold running water. Dry with paper towels. § Detach the stems and slice them in half lengthwise. Make small slits with a sharp knife in the caps and stems and insert the garlic and thyme. Make at least 4 slits per cap and 2 per stem. § Mix the oil, salt, and pepper in a small bowl and drizzle it over the mushrooms. Set aside for a few minutes. § Place the butter, garlic, scallions, parsley, salt, and pepper in a small bowl and mix until smooth. Set aside. § Heat a grill pan to very hot and place the mushrooms in it, beginning with the stems (which may take a little longer to cook, depending on the type of mushroom). § Cook for 5–7 minutes, turning often so they don't stick. § Prepare slices of toast made with whole-wheat or homemade bread, spread with the herb butter, and distribute the mushrooms on top. § Serve immediately as an appetizer or snack.

■ INGREDIENTS

• 1½ lb (750 g) whole fresh wild mushrooms (shiitake, chanterelle, hedgehog, cremini, portobello)
• 4 cloves garlic, sliced
• 4 tablespoons fresh or 2 tablespoons dried thyme
• salt and freshly ground black pepper
• 4 tablespoons extra-virgin olive oil
• ½ cup (4 oz/125 g) butter, softened
• 1 clove garlic, finely chopped
• 1 tablespoon scallions, finely chopped
• 2 tablespoons parsley, finely chopped

Wine: a dry red
(Chianti Classico Aziano)

SPIEDINI DI CIPOLLINE E ALLORO
Skewered grilled onions with bay leaves

Serves: 4; Preparation: 10 minutes; Cooking: 20 minutes; Level of difficulty: Simple

Blanch the onions in a pot of salted, boiling water for 5 minutes. § Drain, dry, and thread onto 4 skewers (5 onions each, alternated with a half bay leaf). Skewer the onions horizontally so that they will lie flat in the grill pan during cooking. § Drizzle with oil and cook in a hot grill pan, turning often. Cook for about 15 minutes, or until the onions are golden brown. § Sprinkle with salt and pepper and serve as appetizers, or with sausages.

■ INGREDIENTS

• 20 small white onions, peeled
• 8 bay leaves, cut in half
• 1 tablespoon extra-virgin olive oil
• salt and freshly ground black pepper

Wine: a dry red (Pinot Nero)

Right: *Spiedini di cipolline e alloro*

Peperoni bruciati
Grilled bell peppers in garlic, parsley, and oil

*Preparing this delicious dish takes a little time, but is definitely worth the effort.
The grilled bell peppers will keep in the refrigerator for about 6 days (cover well with oil),
so you can double or even triple the quantities given here.*

Serves: 4; Preparation: 1 hour; Cooking: 30 minutes; Level of difficulty: Simple

Heat the grill pan to very hot. Place as many whole peppers in the pan as will fit and press down with a lid. The skins of the peppers must burn completely black. Turn them when one side is black. The peppers become soft as they cook; turn them often as they soften to avoid burning the pulp. § Wrap each cooked pepper in 2–3 layers of paper towels (they are easier to peel if kept warm). § When all the peppers are cooked, remove the blackened skins with your fingers and paper towels. § Remove the core, stem, seeds, and filaments. § Flatten the cleaned pieces and cut them into strips. § Place them on a serving dish and dress with the garlic, capers, basil, mint, salt, and plenty of oil. § Mix carefully and set aside for at least 1 hour before serving. § Serve as an appetizer with slices of toasted whole-wheat bread.

■ INGREDIENTS

- 5 large, fleshy, fresh bell peppers (capsicums) of different colors
- 5 cloves garlic, thinly sliced
- ½ cup (2 oz/60 g) capers
- 20 fresh basil leaves, cut into strips
- 15 mint leaves, whole
- salt
- ½ cup (4 fl oz/125 ml) extra-virgin olive oil

*Wine: a dry red
(Recioto di Valpolicella)*

Cipolle grigliate con formaggio dolce fresco
Grilled onions filled with fresh creamy cheese

*If you have an open fire or barbecue, bury the onions in the hot coals or ashes for about 35
minutes. They will have an even more delicious, smoky flavor.*

Serves: 4; Preparation: 10 minutes; Cooking: 45 minutes; Level of difficulty: Simple

Trim the onions top and bottom, taking a larger slice from the top. § Wrap each onion in a piece of aluminum foil. § Heat the grill pan over high heat until very hot. Place the onions in it and lower heat to medium so that the onions cook slowly. Turn from time to time. § After about 45 minutes, pierce an onion through the center with a wooden skewer. If it goes in easily, the onions are done; if the center still feels hard or moist continue cooking for 5–10 minutes. § Remove from the grill and cut in half, season with oil, salt, and pepper, and place half a tablespoon of cheese in each half. § Serve hot with barbecued pork chops or sausages.

■ INGREDIENTS

- 8 medium red or white onions
- 4 tablespoons extra-virgin olive oil
- salt and freshly ground black pepper
- ½ cup (4 oz/125 g) creamy, slightly sweet cheese (Robiola, Mascarpone)

*Wine: a dry red
(Leverano)*

Right: *Cipolle grigliate
con formaggio dolce fresco*

INGREDIENTS

- 4 eggplants (aubergines)
- 4 bell peppers (capsicums)
- 6 ripe tomatoes
- 3 cloves garlic, finely chopped
- ½ cup (4 fl oz/125 ml) extra-virgin olive oil
- salt and freshly ground black pepper
- 10 fresh basil leaves, torn

Wine: a dry white (Soave)

INSALATA GRIGLIATA
Grilled salad

Serves: 6; Preparation: 10 minutes; Cooking: 45 minutes; Level of difficulty: Simple

Cut the eggplants in ½-in (1-cm) thick slices with their skins. § Heat the grill pan to very hot and cook the eggplants until tender. Set aside. § Cut the bell peppers in strips and cook in the grill pan, turning with a fork until they are cooked. Set aside. § Peel the tomatoes, cut them in half, and cook in the grill pan until they are pulpy. § Chop the eggplants and bell peppers in squares and place in a salad bowl with the tomatoes. § Sprinkle with salt, pepper, basil, garlic, and oil and toss.

Salads

Traditional Italian cuisine includes a plethora of delicious salads, from simple green and mixed dishes served after the main course to revive the palate, to more original regional salads, such as fava beans and Pecorino cheese in Tuscany, and green salads with oranges in the citrus-growing south.

Pinzimonio

Platter of raw vegetables with oil, salt, and pepper dip

Pinzimonio is a sort of do-it-yourself-salad. A platter of the season's raw vegetables, washed and cut into manageable pieces, is placed at the center of the table and each guest is given a tiny bowl of oil, salt, and pepper to dip the vegetables. Serve it as an appetizer with slices of toasted whole-wheat or homemade bread or as a refreshing course in itself after a hearty meat dish. These are the traditional pinzimonio vegetables, but use your imagination and whatever you have available in the pantry or garden. Raw zucchini sticks, sliced bell peppers, cherry tomatoes, or cubes of cucumber (with toothpicks for dipping) are just a few that spring to mind.

Serves: 4; Preparation: 20 minutes; Level of difficulty: Simple

Wash all the vegetables thoroughly under cold running water. § Artichokes: remove all but the pale inner leaves by pulling the outer ones down and snapping them off. Cut off the stem and the top third of the remaining leaves. Cut the artichokes in half lengthwise and scrape any fuzzy choke away with a knife. Cut each artichoke in wedges and soak in a bowl of cold water with the juice of 1 lemon for 15 minutes. § Carrots: scrub with a brush or peel and soak in a bowl of cold water with the remaining lemon juice for 10 minutes. § Celery: discard the stringy outer stalks and trim off the leafy tops. Keep the inner white stalks and the heart. § Fennel: slice off the base, trim away the leafy tops, and discard the blemished outer leaves. Divide into 4 or more wedges, depending on the size. § Scallions: remove the roots and the outer leaves and trim the tops. § Radishes: cut the roots off and trim the tops. § For the dip: blend the oil with salt and pepper to taste with a whisk or blender. Pour into 4 small bowls.

INGREDIENTS

- 4 artichokes
- juice of 2 lemons
- 4 carrots (or 8 baby spring carrots)
- 4 celery hearts
- 2 large fennel bulbs
- 12 scallions
- 12 radishes
- 1¾ cups (14 fl oz/ 450 ml) extra-virgin olive oil
- salt and freshly ground black pepper
- 1 tablespoon oregano (optional)

Wine: a light, dry white (Verzemino)

Bagna Cauda

Hot Piedmont-style dip for raw vegetables

Serves: 4-6; Preparation: 10 minutes; Cooking: 25 minutes; Level of difficulty: Simple

Place the garlic in a small pot with a pat of butter and a tablespoon of water. Simmer over very low heat, gradually adding all the butter; make sure the butter doesn't brown or the garlic fry. § Add the anchovy fillets and the oil, a little at a time. Mix well. § The dip is kept hot on the table in an earthenware pot over a warming apparatus (lacking all else, use a candle!). § Serve as a dip for raw vegetables. It is also good with cooked vegetables, roast bell peppers, and as a sauce for fresh pasta and potato gnocchi.

INGREDIENTS

- 6 cloves garlic, very finely chopped
- ¼ cup (2 oz/60 g) butter
- ¾ cup (7 fl oz/200 ml) extra-virgin olive oil
- 20 anchovy fillets (best if packed under salt), finely chopped

Right:
Insalata aranciata

INGREDIENTS

- 3 fresh oranges
- 5 oz (150 g) arugula
  (rocket)
- 5 oz (150 g) corn salad
- 2 medium red onions
- 1 cup (3½ oz/100 g)
  black olives, pitted and
  chopped
- ⅓ cup (3½ fl oz/100 ml)
  extra-virgin olive oil
- ⅓ cup (3½ fl oz/100 ml)
  red vinegar
- salt and black pepper

INSALATA ARANCIATA
Arugula and oranges with olives and sweet red onions

Serves: 6; Preparation: 20 minutes; Level of difficulty: Simple

Peel the oranges, discard any seeds and use a sharp knife to remove all the white part. Cut in thick slices and divide each slice in half. § Wash and dry the salad greens. § Cut the onions in thin slices. § Place the oranges, arugula, corn salad, onions, and olives in a salad bowl. § Mix the oil, vinegar, salt and pepper together in bowl and pour over the salad. Toss well. § Set aside for 20 minutes before serving. § Serve as an appetizer with toasted whole-wheat or homemade bread.

Insalata di spinaci e grana
Raw spinach and Parmesan salad

Serves: 4; Preparation: 15 minutes; Level of difficulty: Simple

Trim the stems and discard any bruised spinach leaves, wash thoroughly, drain and dry on a clean cotton dish towel. § Grate the carrots in julienne strips. § Place the spinach in a large round dish or low, wide salad bowl and sprinkle with the carrots and corn. § Top with the flakes of Parmesan. § In a small bowl, dissolve the salt in the lemon juice, add the oil and pepper, and whisk to blend. § Dress the salad 5 minutes before serving. § This salad makes an eyecatching appetizer, but can also be served as a side dish with barbecued or braised meats.

> VARIATION
> – Add a small honeydew melon in balls (made with a melon baller) or cubes, and 5 oz (150 g) of lean prosciutto in strips.

■ INGREDIENTS

- 7 cups dwarf spinach, tender and very fresh
- 2 carrots, peeled
- 1 cup (4 oz/125 g) canned corn kernels, or 8 baby corn cobs
- 1¼ cups (4 oz/125 g) Parmesan cheese, in flakes
- ½ teaspoon salt
- juice of 1 lemon
- 4 tablespoons extra-virgin olive oil
- freshly ground black pepper

Wine: a dry white (Biondello del Metauro)

Asparagi in insalata
Asparagus salad

This tasty salad is also good with mayonnaise (see recipe p. 28)

Serves: 4; Preparation: 20 minutes; Cooking: 10 minutes; Level of difficulty: Simple

Trim the tough parts off the asparagus stalks and blanch for 7–10 minutes in a pot of salted, boiling water. Drain well and set aside to cool. § Wash and dry the radicchio and detach the leaves. § Arrange a bed of radicchio leaves on a serving dish and scatter with the mushrooms. Arrange the asparagus on top. § Dissolve the salt in the lemon juice and add the lemon peel and basil, oil, and pepper, and blend thoroughly. § Pour the dressing over the salad and serve as a light lunch with sliced hard-cooked eggs, tuna, and anchovy fillets.

■ INGREDIENTS

- 2 lb (1 kg) asparagus
- 6 heads red radicchio
- 3 cups (12 oz/375 g) white mushrooms, thinly sliced
- ½ teaspoon salt
- peel of 2 lemons, finely chopped with 10 basil leaves
- ⅓ cup (3½ fl oz/100 ml) extra-virgin olive oil
- 3 tablespoons lemon juice
- freshly ground black pepper

Wine: a dry white (Gambellara)

Right: Insalata di spinaci e grana

INSALATA DI FAGIOLINI CON IL PANE FRITTO
Green bean salad with fried bread

Serves: 4; Preparation: 20 minutes; Cooking: 15 minutes; Level of difficulty: Simple

Cut the tips off the beans, cut in half, wash and cook in a pot of salted, boiling water for 7–8 minutes, or until tender. Drain, dry on paper towels, and place in a large salad bowl. § Sauté the bacon in a small skillet with 1 tablespoon of oil until crisp. Drain and set aside. § Fry the bread in a pan with 4 tablespoons of oil and the garlic, remove when golden brown, and drain on paper towels. § In a small bowl, dissolve the salt in the lemon juice, and add the pepper, oregano, parsley, scallions, and remaining oil. Dress the salad, sprinkle with the capers, and toss with the cubes of bread. § Serve as a light lunch, or as a side dish with barbecued meat.

> VARIATION
> – To make the salad more complete, add a simple omelet (4 eggs for 4 people). Beat the eggs with salt and pepper and cook in a large skillet so that it forms a thin layer. Cool and dice and toss with the salad.

■ INGREDIENTS

- 1 lb (500 g) green beans
- salt and black pepper
- 2 bunches chives, finely chopped
- 1¾ cups (7 oz/210 g) bacon, diced
- ⅔ cup (5 fl oz/150 ml) extra-virgin olive oil
- 5 1-in (2.5-cm)-thick slices firm-textured bread, cut in cubes
- 1 large clove garlic, cut in quarters
- juice of 2 lemons
- 1 tablespoon oregano
- 1 tablespoon parsley, finely chopped
- 8 scallions (spring onions), chopped
- 2 tablespoons capers

Wine: a dry white (Riesling Italico)

INSALATA ALLEGRA
Summer salad greens with strawberries and apples

Serves: 4; Preparation: 20 minutes; Level of difficulty: Simple

Blend the oil, chives, salt, and pepper with a whisk. Set aside for 20 minutes. § Wash and dry the salad greens. Arrange a bed of mixed salad leaves in four individual salad bowls. § Wash the apples thoroughly, divide in half, remove the core and cut in thin wedges, without peeling. § Arrange a ring of apple wedges over the salad in each bowl. § Scatter the sliced radishes over the apples. § Cut the strawberries in half and garnish each salad, placing a teaspoonful of Ricotta between each strawberry. § Pour the dressing over each plate. § Serve with crusty fresh bread or toast as an appetizer.

■ INGREDIENTS

- ¼ cup (2 fl oz/60 ml) extra-virgin olive oil
- 2 tablespoons chives, chopped
- salt and freshly ground black pepper
- 13 oz (400 g) corn salad or green cutting lettuce
- 6 oz (200 g) red and green ryegrass or curly endive hearts
- 2 Red Delicious apples
- 10 red radishes, sliced
- 14 oz (350 g) firm ripe strawberries
- 1½ cups (12 oz/350 g) Ricotta cheese

Wine: a dry white (Colli Albani)

Right: *Insalata allegra*

Insalatina di bosco con riso selvatico
Woodland salad with raspberries and wild rice

Serves: 4; Preparation: 20 minutes; Cooking: 40 minutes; Level of difficulty: Simple

Cook the rice in a pot of salted, boiling water for about 40 minutes, or until cooked. § Wash and dry the mixed salad greens. § Prepare the vinaigrette. Crush about 15 raspberries and add to the dressing. Blend well. § Place the salad greens in a large salad bowl (or 4 individual bowls), add the herbs, and toss well. § Sprinkle with the carrot and pour half the vinaigrette over the top. Garnish with 20 raspberries. § Drain the rice, shaking thoroughly to remove excess moisture. Transfer to a bowl and mix well with the oil. § Place in a large serving dish (or 4 individual bowls) and garnish with the remaining raspberries. Drizzle with the rest of the vinaigrette. § Serve the salad with the rice as an entrée or light lunch, or as a main course with grilled sole or bass, or with poached eggs.

Insalata di lenticchie e odori
Lentil and herb salad

Serves: 4; Preparation: 20 minutes; Cooking: 45 minutes; Level of difficulty: Simple

Cook the lentils with the onion (with the cloves stuck in it), thyme, bay leaves, and carrots in a large pan of salted water for about 45 minutes. § Check the carrots during cooking and remove as soon as they are soft (which will be before the lentils are ready). § Drain the lentils, shaking well to remove excess moisture, and transfer a salad bowl. Discard the bay leaves, thyme, and cloves. § Cut the onion in thin slices and dice the carrots and add to the lentils. § While still hot, season with oil, salt, vinegar, and pepper, and mix well. § Add the chopped garlic and parsley and mix again. Set aside for 5 minutes. § Serve as an entrée, or as a side dish with broiled sausages.

■ INGREDIENTS

- ¾ cup (5 oz/150 g) brown rice
- ⅔ cup (4 oz/140 g) wild black or red rice
- 1 lb (500 g) mixed wild salad greens (dandelion, wild endives and green radicchio)
- 2 quantities *Vinagrette* (see recipe p. 24)
- 2 cups (1 lb/500 g) fresh raspberries
- 1 bunch arugula, cut finely with scissors
- 1 bunch salad burnet
- 15 fresh mint leaves
- 1 bunch fresh chervil, in sprigs
- 2 bunches cress, coarsely chopped
- 4 carrots, finely grated
- 4 tablespoons extra-virgin olive oil

Wine: a dry red (Capri)

■ INGREDIENTS

- 1 lb (500 g) lentils, soaked in water overnight
- 1 large onion
- 2 cloves
- 1 sprig fresh thyme
- 5 bay leaves
- 3 large carrots
- salt and black pepper
- ⅓ cup (3½ fl oz/100 ml) extra-virgin olive oil
- 2 tablespoons red wine vinegar
- 4 cloves garlic, 4 sprigs parsley, finely chopped

Wine: a dry red (Nebbiola d'Alba)

Right: *Insalatina di bosco con riso selvatico*

Pomodoro al tonno
Tomatoes filled with tuna and mayonnaise

Serves: 4; Preparation: 30 minutes; Level of difficulty: Simple

Wash the tomatoes and cut a ¼-in (6-mm) slice off the top of each. Hollow them out with a knife and teaspoon (be careful not to break the skin). Place them upside down on a plate to drain for 10 minutes. § Sprinkle the insides with salt and pepper. § Prepare the mayonnaise. § In a bowl, squash the egg yolks with a fork and mix with 2 tablespoons of mayonnaise. Add the olives, anchovies, capers, tuna, and parsley. Mix well, adding mayonnaise as you go. § Chop the egg whites and add them to the mixture. Keep mixing with the fork. Add pepper to taste. § Use a teaspoon to fill the tomatoes. Place a teaspoon of mayonnaise on the top of each and garnish with 2–3 capers and basil leaves. § Place the filled tomatoes in the bottom of the refrigerator for 20 minutes. § Serve as an entrée or light lunch with torn lettuce leaves dressed with oil and lemon and toasted whole-wheat or homemade bread.

■ INGREDIENTS

- 8 medium ripe tomatoes
- salt and freshly ground black pepper
- 4 hard-cooked eggs
- 2 quantities *Mayonnaise* (see recipe p. 24)
- 6 green olives, pitted and finely chopped
- 6 anchovy fillets, chopped
- ⅓ cup (1½ oz/45 g) capers (half this quantity finely chopped, rest whole to garnish)
- 2 cups (1 lb/500 g) tuna in olive oil, chopped
- 1 tablespoon parsley, finely chopped
- 16 fresh basil leaves

Wine: a dry white (Montescudaio)

Insalata di pecorino e baccelli
Tuscan fava bean and Pecorino cheese salad

This salad is best in early spring when fava beans are just beginning to be appear in the shops. They should be fresh and tender from the earliest picking.

Serves: 4; Preparation: 20 minutes; Level of difficulty: Simple

Shell the fava beans and place in a large slightly concave dish. § Dice the Pecorino and mix with the beans. Add pepper, a sprinkling of salt, and the oil. § Mix well and serve the salad as an appetizer by itself or with a platter of cold meats such as prosciutto, ham, and salami.

■ INGREDIENTS

- 3 lb (1.5 kg) small, fresh fava (broad) beans in their pods
- 10 oz (300 g) fresh young Pecorino cheese
- salt and freshly ground black pepper
- 4 tablespoons extra-virgin olive oil

Wine: a dry red (Chianti dei Colli Senesi)

VARIATIONS
— Add the juice of ½ a lemon and 1½ cups of diced prosciutto.
— Add two peeled and diced sweet pears.

Right:
Insalata di pecorino e baccelli

■ INGREDIENTS

• half a medium white or
  red Savoy cabbage
• 2 sweet red onions
• 1 Golden Delicious apple
• 2 quantities *Vinaigrette*
  (see recipe p. 24)

Wine: a dry sparkling white
(Trebbianino Val Trebbia)

Insalata di verza e cipolla
Cabbage and onion salad

Serves: 4; Preparation: 15 minutes; Level of difficulty: Simple

Cut the cabbage in thin strips and slice the onions thinly. Toss well together. § Peel and core the apples, dice and add to the cabbage. § Prepare the vinagrette and pour over the salad. § Toss well and set aside for 10–15 minutes before serving with barbecued pork chops or fried chicken.

VARIATION
– Replace the vinaigrette with 2 quantities of homemade mayonnaise (see recipe p. 24).

- 2 large heads red radicchio
- 2 hearts curly endive, chopped
- 1 14-oz (450 g) can red kidney beans
- 16 shrimp, shelled
- salt and freshly ground black pepper
- ½ cup (4 fl oz/125 g) extra-virgin olive oil
- ⅓ cup (3½ fl oz/100 ml) white wine vinegar
- grated rind of ½ a lemon
- 4 scallions (spring onions), finely chopped
- 1 celery heart, finely chopped

Wine: a dry white (Falerio dei colli Ascolani)

INSALATA DI GAMBERI E FAGIOLI
Shrimp and red bean salad

Serves: 4; Preparation: 30 minutes; Cooking: 5 minutes; Level of difficulty: Simple

Wash and dry the salad vegetables. § Strip the red leaves from the radicchio and arrange in 4 small salad bowls. § Distribute the endive over the radicchio leaves. Chop the radicchio hearts and arrange over the endive. § Drain the beans and distribute in the 4 bowls over the salad. § Heat 2 tablespoons of oil in a skillet and sauté the shrimp with a little salt over high heat for 2 minutes. § Add the wine vinegar with the lemon peel and cook for 3–4 minutes more. § Place the remaining oil, with salt, pepper, scallions, and celery in a bowl and beat vigorously with a fork. § Divide the shrimp, 4 in each salad bowl, and pour the oil over the top. § Serve at once as an entrée (prepare grilled fish to follow), or as a second course preceded by a shellfish risotto.

VARIATION
– A simpler version can be made with white beans and shrimp cooked in salted, boiling water for 3 minutes and seasoned with extra-virgin olive oil, salt, freshly ground black pepper, and 2 tablespoons of finely chopped parsley.

INSALATA CAPRESE
Tomato and Mozzarella cheese

- 7 large red tomatoes
- 1 lb (500 g) Mozzarella cheese
- 20 large basil leaves
- salt and freshly ground black pepper
- ⅓ cup (3½ fl oz/100 ml) extra-virgin olive oil

Wine: a dry white (Cinque Terre)

Serves: 4; Preparation: 15 minutes; Level of difficulty: Simple

Cut the tomatoes in ¼-in (6-mm) thick slices and arrange on a flat serving dish. § Cut the Mozzarella in slices of the same width and alternate with the tomato. § Sprinkle with basil, salt, and pepper, and drizzle with the oil. § Serve as an entrée or light lunch (with lots of crusty fresh bread).

VARIATION
– For a tastier salad, sprinkle with 2 teaspoons of dried oregano.

Left: Insalata caprese

Insalata di farro
Spelt salad

Spelt has been grown in Italy for thousands of years. It is used in Italian cuisine for salads and soups. Look for it in specialty shops, or try replacing it with pearl barley. This delicious salad looks particularly appetizing when served in a wooden bowl. To give it even more color and flavor, add 4 raw diced courgettes and 8 crumbled anchovy fillets.

Serves: 4; Preparation: 15 minutes; Cooking: 40 minutes; Level of difficulty: Simple

Cook the spelt in a pot of salted, boiling water. The cooking time will depend on the freshness of the grain, so try a couple of grains after 40 minutes; it should be chewy but firm. § Drain and rinse under cold running water. Drain again and shake out excess moisture. § Transfer to a bowl. § Add the tomatoes, Mozzarella, scallions, basil, capers, salt, pepper, and oil, mix well and set aside for 5–10 minutes before serving. Put extra olive oil on the table with the salad because the spelt is very absorbent and may require more. § Serve as an entrée.

■ INGREDIENTS

- 3½ cups (1 lb/500 g) spelt
- salt and freshly ground black pepper
- 16 cherry tomatoes, cut in half
- 2 cups (1 lb/500 g) Mozzarella cheese, diced
- 6 scallions (spring onions), chopped
- 15 basil leaves, cut in strips with scissors
- ⅓ cup (1½ oz/45 g) capers
- ⅓ cup (3½ fl oz/100 ml) extra-virgin olive oil

*Wine: a dry white
(Vernaccia di San Gimignano)*

Insalata di cuori con salmone
Salad hearts with smoked salmon

Serves: 4; Preparation: 20 minutes; Cooking: 7-8 minutes; Level of difficulty: Simple

Wash the salad greens and dry on a clean cotton dish towel. § Remove all but the pale inner leaves from the artichokes by pulling the outer ones down and snapping them off. Cut off the stem and the top third of the remaining leaves until only the tender heart remains. Cut the artichokes in half lengthwise and scrape any fuzzy choke away with a knife. Cut each heart in half and cook in a pot of salted, boiling water with the juice of 1 lemon for 7–8 minutes, or until they are white and tender. Drain and set aside to cool. § Dissolve ½ teaspoon of salt in the remaining lemon juice, add the oil and pepper, and mix well. § Place the lettuce, endive, celery, palm hearts, and scallions in a bowl and season with the dressing (leave a little for the artichoke hearts). § Mix well and arrange the salad in 4 plates. Place the artichoke hearts at the center of each and drizzle with the remaining dressing. § Garnish the 4 bowls with the salmon. § Serve as an entrée with toasted whole-wheat or homemade bread.

■ INGREDIENTS

- 2 heads lettuce, divided in leaves
- 4 large artichoke hearts
- salt and freshly ground black pepper
- juice of 2 lemons
- ¼ cup (3½ fl oz/100 ml) extra-virgin olive oil
- 1 large head Belgian endive, thinly sliced
- 2 celery hearts, chopped
- 4 palm hearts, sliced into thick wheels
- 4 scallions, chopped
- 12 oz (350 g) smoked salmon, thinly sliced

*Wine: a dry, aromatic white
(Pigato)*

Right:
Insalata di farro

■ INGREDIENTS

- 10 cups green radicchio
- 1½ cups (6 oz/250 g) pancetta, diced
- 2½ tablespoons red wine vinegar
- 4 tablespoons extra-virgin olive oil
- salt and freshly ground black pepper

Wine: a dry, sparkling red (Lambrusco)

Radicchio verde alla pancetta croccante
Green radicchio with crispy-fried pancetta

Serves: 4; Preparation: 25 minutes; Cooking: 5 minutes; Level of difficulty: Simple

Discard any wilted leaves from the radicchio, trim the stems, wash thoroughly, drain and dry. § Sauté the pancetta in a skillet without oil (it produces enough of its own). Add the vinegar and cook until the pancetta is crisp. Remove from heat. § Season the radicchio with oil, salt, pepper, and vinegar and sprinkle the pancetta over the top. Toss well. § Serve with hard-cooked eggs and toasted homemade bread rubbed with garlic.

Insalata di Carciofi
Artichoke salad

■ INGREDIENTS

• 5 large fresh artichokes
• juice of 2 lemons
• 2 dashes salt and freshly ground black pepper
• ⅓ cup (3½ fl oz/100 ml) extra-virgin olive oil
• 2 tablespoons parsley, finely chopped
• 2 tablespoons mint leaves, finely chopped

Wine: a dry white
(Trebbiano di Romagna)

Serves: 4; Preparation: 25 minutes; Level of difficulty: Simple

Remove all but the pale inner leaves from the artichokes by pulling the outer ones down and snapping them off. Cut off the stem and the top third of the remaining leaves. Cut the artichokes in half lengthwise and scrape any fuzzy choke away with a knife. Cut each artichoke in wedges and soak in a bowl of cold water with the juice of 1 lemon for 10 minutes. § Dissolve the salt in the remaining lemon juice. Add the oil, pepper, parsley, and mint and beat vigorously to emulsify. § Cut the artichokes in thin slices, pour the dressing over the top, and toss well. § Serve as an appetizer, or as a side dish with barbecued meat or fish.

Insalata cotta di verdura miste
Cooked mixed vegetable salad

■ INGREDIENTS

• 5 bulbs fennel
• 5 artichokes
• 6 medium carrots
• 6 long zucchini (courgettes)
• 6 medium potatoes
• 6 beets
• 1 lb (500 g) green beans
• 1 quantity *Mayonnaise* (see recipe p. 24) or 1 quantity *Vinaigrette* (see recipe p. 24)

Wine: a dry red
(Chianti dei Colli Aretini)

A classic of Italian cookery, Insalata cotta *is nearly always on the menu in any restaurant or trattoria, and is served in most homes at least once a week. The secret lies in the dressing, either homemade mayonnaise or extra-virgin oil and vinegar (or lemon juice). You can vary the vegetables according to the season or what you have on hand.*

Serves: 4-6; Preparation: 25 minutes; Cooking: 25 minutes; Level of difficulty: Simple

Cook all the vegetables whole in abundant salted, boiling water until they are just tender. You can cook them all together if you wish, removing the different vegetables as they are ready. The beets will stain the other vegetables, so you might want to cook them apart. § Peel the potatoes and beets after cooking. To peel the beets, just press the skin with your fingers and it will slip off easily. § When all the vegetables are cooked, drain well and arrange (either sliced or whole) on a large tray, divided by types. § Serve warm with vinaigrette, mayonnaise, or a little lemon juice and olive oil. § In Italy this cooked salad is served as a side dish with roast meat or fish, or hard-cooked eggs and canned tuna.

Right:
Insalata cotta di verdure miste

Index